T0207620

PURE LOVE

Pursuing Purity in a Sex-Obsessed World

TIMON BENGTSON & SARAH ROSE

WESTBOW
P R E S S®
A DIVISION OF THOMAS NELSON
& ZONDERVAN

WestBow Press books may be ordered through booksellers or by contacting:

WestBow Press
A Division of Thomas Nelson & Zondervan
1663 Liberty Drive
Bloomington, IN 47403
www.westbowpress.com
1 (866) 928-1240

ISBN: 978-1-5127-0670-3 (sc)
ISBN: 978-1-5127-0671-0 (hc)
ISBN: 978-1-5127-0669-7 (e)

Library of Congress Control Number: 2015912658

Print information available on the last page.

WestBow Press rev. date: 9/2/2015

For the young adults of
CityReach Baptist Church

May your lives be ruled by the Gospel,
And your hearts captivated by His love

ACKNOWLEDGEMENTS

This book has been the culmination of many hours of help, discussion and support from many people.

Thank you.

To Gill Preston, who spent hours of her own time editing our book. Thank you for your insight, advice and professionalism. Our book is better because of you.

To Andrew and Jeremy for your collaboration, and contribution to this book.

To Sara, Fabio, Dan, Emily, Kerri and Matt who read our drafts and gave us feedback and encouragement.

To Les for your meticulous drafting, insight, wisdom and sound theology.

To Luke for your hours of proofreading.

To the CityReach Baptist Church who encouraged us, prayed for us and released us to do this book.

To the CityReach Eldership who supported the vision and encouraged us with their wisdom.

To Tiana who spent hours working on our graphics and cover design.

To Tegan, Hannah, Abbey, Emma, Ava and Bella, my precious family, for their ongoing support.

And to our great God, from whom comes all wisdom. Without Your love and Your grace there would have been nothing to write. May this book, and our lives, bring You glory.

CONTENTS

INTRODUCTION

Evelyn's Story

I never thought this would be my story. I had hoped that mine would be different, that I would live a different way. But, I had a lot to learn.

It sounds like a cliché, but I was raised by wonderful Christian parents who taught my siblings and me from as early as I can remember who the Lord Jesus was and what it meant to be his follower. I remember having a strong desire from a young age to serve him, to live my whole life for Him. As I grew older I made commitments to keep my heart and life pure, in particular from sexual sin. I wore the purity rings, I signed the declarations and I counselled other young women who were struggling in their relationships; I resolved that I would stand firm.

While many of the big temptations that threaten sexual purity have touched my life in one way or another, it wasn't these that were my undoing. It was the subtle messages that many of us carry through life that led me to be vulnerable when it really counted. The message that:

- ○ *if you are single there is something wrong with you*
- ○ *men are only attracted to women who are emotionally and sexually confident*
- ○ *true love is the ultimate fulfilment of who we should be*
- ○ *we are sexual beings who can't help but express those desires.*

Sin is deceptive and cunning in its approach, and I'm sure this is why so many of us fall. I was a strong, determined woman with experience (both good and bad) at protecting myself from sexual sin, yet in the end it was my self-righteousness that led me to sin and heartache. I hadn't prepared myself for my own heart and mind to lead me astray; I hadn't factored in my convictions loosening and shifting.

I was in love. I had entered this relationship with prayer and confidence that the Lord had opened this door for us. There were a few issues, to be sure. He was only months into his return to the Lord, after many years of walking his own way, but I knew that if we kept Christ central in our relationship, and took things slowly, we could have a great future together. At first this is what we did. We talked for hours about the Lord, we read His Word together and prayed, but soon we began to spend more time together doing other things and less time in God's Word. I didn't notice it at first, but when we began to differ in some of our opinions, my faith and resolves were already weakening.

Over the next few months as my feelings for him grew, my heart and mind started to justify different parts of our relationship. Subtle changes in my convictions led my whole life to be thrown off balance. I was still involved in ministry, but my conviction wasn't there. I was still walking the walk, but my resolve and my impact were weakened. When our relationship wasn't going as well as I had hoped, and our beliefs about God grew further and further apart, I decided that I wanted this relationship more than anything else, and that I would do anything to make it work. This is when we started sleeping together. I wanted him to want me, and so I gave him everything that I could. I tried everything; I became whatever he wanted me to be. I didn't want to lose the future I had pictured, the hopes I had and the dreams I had so longed for. And in giving him everything, I lost everything. I lost my identity, my hope, my security and my faith. He couldn't give me anything in return, and so within months it was over.

And there I found myself, broken and alone, with no idea how I had fallen so far. I had been a leader and a counsellor, determined to stand against this type of sin, and yet, like so many others, I had let my desires rule and pushed God into the background...

When I (Sarah) first heard this story, I was shaken. I was hit hard with the humbling reality that none of us, no matter how strong we think we stand, are immune to the deceptiveness of sin, or our own sinful hearts.

We live in a world in which sexual immorality is promoted and glorified at every turn, and tragically, as God's people, many of us fall prey, daily, to its seduction. Precious people, redeemed by Jesus' blood give into temptation and are consumed with guilt. They go to church, engage in corporate worship, and may even serve in a ministry of the church, but beneath it all they are consumed with sexual and relational sin. The Spirit of God is grieved when we live our own way, even as we pretend to be following Him. The very church that has been equipped to be the light of the world is languishing under the pressure of darkness, its impact quenched. The stakes are high and from where we are sitting it seems like the church in the west is losing the fight.

Why a book on sexual purity?

This book came about because, in my (Timon's) pastoral ministry, I began to realize that this is not just an issue that some people struggle with—everyone struggles with it. And there is a good reason for this. The world that my grandfather grew up in is a completely different world to the one that my children inhabit.

In the 1930s and 40s the majority of Australian society embraced basic Christian morals. This meant that the church did not have to be very intentional at discipling its people in sexual ethics and relationships because the foundational institutions of our society—government, media, school and family—were essentially affirming what the church taught in these areas. The church and our society were basically swimming in the same direction.

However, the current started to shift after the Second World War with the sexual revolution. No longer did the majority of Australians believe that sex should be reserved for marriage. No longer was pornography relegated to the seedy part of town. The tide was starting to turn. And the church found that she was swimming upstream.

Since the 1960s the current has been getting stronger and shows no signs of changing direction. What was once considered to be pornography is now a part of most major motion pictures and television shows. More extreme forms of porn are now readily accessible on the Internet and the industry has reshaped how men and women think about sex. Homosexuality, which used to be outlawed in most states of Australia, is now not only acceptable and legal, but is celebrated as good and healthy. Sex outside of marriage has become the norm, and even one night stands are considered to be not only okay, but even healthy. The 'try before you buy' philosophy has overtaken sexual purity as the best pathway to having great sex when you do finally settle down.

So, how has the church responded in general to this changing environment? For the most part, we have been caught sleeping. In most of the churches that I have been a member, sexual ethics and relationships were rarely addressed. We would have the standard talk about sexual purity, but topics like sex, dating, singleness, pornography, masturbation and homosexually were never discussed. What this means is that most Christians, and in particular, most Christian young people, are getting their cues about sexuality from their culture.

Many young Christians see little need to be drastically different from the culture. Even Christians who *do* desire sexual purity are often not well equipped to deal with the full on sexual temptation that is now a part of everyday life in the western world. Whenever a young man comes to me for discipleship I have learned to assume that one of his struggles (sadly often a losing struggle) will be with pornography and masturbation.

The struggles within relationships and the battle for sexual purity are consuming our young people, and I believe that these may be fundamental reasons why the church in the west is often powerless and not growing.

We have written this book because we believe in the purpose and mission of the church. Every Christian has an important role to play in the church but we can see the drastic ways in which the battle for sexual purity is claiming casualties and crippling entire parts of the body of Christ. We believe the Bible has the answers and that through God's divine power the Christian is supernaturally equipped with everything they need to fight this battle (2 Peter 1:3).

If we are going to turn things around then we need intentional discipleship in this area. This topic needs addressing openly and often if we are going to strengthen people to swim against the ever-growing tide. Christian young people need to understand the influence of the *culture* on various aspects of their sexuality. They need to know the truth of what the *Scripture* says. Finally, they need to understand what they are *called* to do, and how the love and grace of Jesus Christ enables them to follow a call that is becoming increasingly radical.

Sarah and I have collaborated on this project to bring you a resource that is practical and strongly biblical, with insights from each of our unique perspectives. Sometimes in a chapter you'll hear primarily from me and my experiences, while in other chapters you'll hear more from Sarah. We have written each chapter to stand-alone, so it can be a resource for Christian young people, youth leaders and pastors as we all stand together to fight in the battle for sexual purity, the health of the church, and the glory of God.

CHAPTER 1

Dating: Choosing wisely, pursuing intentionally

Sarah Rose (with Andrew Green)

Twenty-year-old Mark walked in the door of his parents' house. It was 2:00 am. All the lights were out except one lamp in the family room and the house was completely still and silent.

He put his keys on the bench, hoping he could make it to his room without losing it, but all of a sudden the full weight of his burden became too much and he burst into tears. As his knees hit the floor, all he could say to himself was 'You're an idiot... Look what you've done'.

After a year in an up-and-down, selfish, dating relationship that was going nowhere, Mark had finally pulled the pin. As he knelt on the floor he knew that he had trodden on someone's heart and deeply wounded her.

Before he knew it, his mum had joined him down on the living room floor in her dressing gown. As she put her arm around him he wept openly saying, 'I've hurt her mum... I've smashed her heart...I'm such an idiot. I hate myself.'

Pain and confusion consumed his mind and the shame of what had happened drilled deep into his heart.

Twelve months earlier it had all started with a young guy feeling flattered by the affection of an attractive girl. The feelings of flattery and a lack of wisdom had led to Mark spending a lot of alone time connecting emotionally with this young woman. He relished being admired and allowed things to go deeper and deeper. He was hearing things he didn't know how to handle and found himself saying things back that he was neither ready to say, nor fully understood.

Mark's eyes were opening wide at the possibilities that came with an attractive girl being interested in him and he flirted with his conscience about the dangerous path of physical intimacy that promised so much—all in the name of 'love'.

Mark had heard a lot of the dating advice that was going around. At the time the book, I Kissed Dating Goodbye *was all the rage, but it was a bit radical for him, and instead he was learning about relationships and how to treat women from the guys at the local football club. Little by little, without realising it, his heart was being deceived to think that his behaviour was normal and would deliver fulfilment.*

But twelve months later, on his living room floor, Mark was anything but fulfilled. He was broken... because it was all a lie.

The culture

Have you ever wondered what's gone wrong with dating? Take a moment to think about it. As you consider the culture that we live in, is it possible, that when it comes to relationships, we're doing it all wrong?

Divorce rates are high, pre-marital sex is the norm, and that's just the beginning. Broken hearts and all-consuming rollercoaster relationships seem par for the course. That's just the way our culture is.

But it's not just in our culture; it's in the church too. And I find myself wondering if maybe God wants us to be doing things differently; if Jesus died to redeem more than just our souls. Maybe He wants to change our lives. Maybe He wants to use us to redeem our culture, but we can't do it until we're living differently. Until our lives don't just meet the status quo, but they show the world that there is another way, and it's God's way, and it's better.

So what's gone wrong with dating? Once we start looking into it, I don't think it's that hard to figure out. We've got it completely disordered: our motives are backwards and our actions are upside down.

How often have you walked into a party, and within the first five minutes made a general assessment of those in the room of the opposite gender based on their physical attractiveness? Those who pass the initial screening process then become the persons of choice to begin to build a conversation or potential relationship with.

This 'relationship' quickly moves into sexual intimacy. In some instances sexual intimacy may follow within hours of the initial attraction. With others it takes a bit longer. Nevertheless 'sexual compatibility' is often held as somewhat of a prerequisite to forming a committed dating relationship.

Once a person has experienced physical and sexual attraction, along with some form of emotional connection, they begin to approach what is all too often the final step in the dating process: friendship, commitment and loyalty.

Can you see how, as a church, we've adopted the world's standards? We've adopted excessive privacy in which young couples drift off the scene, as they become each other's entire worlds. We've adopted unintentionality in which people crash in and out of different dating relationships, while other relationships go nowhere forever.

We've adopted flippancy towards sex and sensuality, getting caught up in the cravings of the world and rejecting God's way as unrealistic. We seek to fulfil our own needs now, rather than patiently waiting to fulfil the needs of someone else when it's time.

We've also adopted the world's views on independence. Self is king, and we don't like to come under the authority of the church. We reject teaching on gender roles because it's unpopular in our modern culture and we take many of our ideals for our future spouse from the world rather than the Bible. We have conformed on screening people *out* who don't fit the 'designer spouse' mould and we've screened people *in* who actually fit in very neatly with the world.

Instead of being motivated by glorifying God, we're motivated by gratifying self. Instead of acting with integrity and giving everything to a person when it's time, we're giving into temptation and taking something before we're ready.

This is not what God intended for us! Stories like Mark's are not God's ideal, but it's more than just about ideals. When you're motivated by self-gratification and pursuing things before you're ready you're actually missing out. You're missing out on the blessing that God has for you when you do things His way and you're missing out on serving Him, unhindered, in ministry.

Jesus did not die so that you can live complacently. He didn't die so that you can jump into the rat race with everyone else, endlessly pursuing your own happiness, but never finding true joy. He came that you may have life, and have it abundantly (John 10:10).

So are you ready for the greater call? Are you ready to live radically and be separate from your culture? Are you ready to stop asking 'What can I get away with?' and start asking 'What can I do to honour God?' Are you ready to give up disordered dating and to submit to God's order?

If you are, then the Bible can show you how.

The Scripture

One of the challenges in looking to the Bible for dating advice is that the word 'dating' is never mentioned. In fact, it's interesting to note that God never gave any specific commands about how to find a spouse. The culture of the Bible was largely dominated by arranged marriages, and while this was the cultural norm, God never presented it as the ideal.

God has not given us an ideal cultural model for pre-marital relationships. He has, however, given many moral principles that enable you to make wise decisions within your individual cultures. The question shouldn't be about whether arranged marriage, courtship or dating is the *right model,* but rather, whether you are living in such a way that your actions bring glory to God.

There are three things that the Bible teaches that will help you to order your dating life:

1) Put God first

This is the number one command for Christians. In everything you do, and every relationship you have, God must always come first.

In Romans 12:1 Paul encourages the believers to 'present [their] bodies as a living sacrifice, holy and acceptable to God which is [their] spiritual worship'.

This is massive! God must be the primary object of our worship and affection, and often agonising over whom to date and how a relationship will progress replaces God in our hearts. It is not wrong to think about these things, but when they replace God our dating becomes disordered. Everything we have, and everything we do, must be laid on the altar in submission to Christ. How often have you agonised over whom to date and how that relationship should progress, when really you just needed to be focusing on loving God with your heart mind and soul?

How many of you really think about putting God first when it comes to relationships? It's a scary thought. If you put God first, He may require things of you that are difficult. He might even make you *wait!* He may take away that person whom you thought was just perfect for you!

He might, but you can be sure that if He does, His ways are perfect and He is a good God who has your best interests at heart.

Putting God first should not be negotiable in the Christian life. In Ephesians, Paul exhorts us to 'walk in a manner worthy of the calling to which you have been called' (Ephesians 4:1). When we look at our calling on this earth it cannot be better summed up than by Jesus' command, that we love the Lord our God with all our heart soul and mind, and that we love our neighbours as ourselves (Matthew 22:37, 39). Our earthly relationships are always to be characterised by a desire to please and honour God first, and then to honour others above ourselves. In Philippians 2:3, we are told to 'do nothing from selfish ambition or conceit, but in humility count others more significant than yourselves'. Relationships that are focused on us fulfilling our needs first, have lost sight of God's order. He desires to bless us, and He does this, not when we are self-seeking, but when we 'seek first the Kingdom of God and His righteousness' (Matthew 6:33).

If you are putting God first, your dating life won't be disordered. You won't be taking something before you're ready, because you'll be focused on emulating Christ in your relationship. You won't be seeking your own enjoyment and gratification as the most important things, but you'll be looking for someone whom you can love and whom you can glorify God together with.

God knows that when you put him first, and pursue others in a godly way, you build relationships and a love that lasts. This love leads not only to deep emotional and spiritual fulfilment, but also to deep sexual fulfilment when the time is right.

2) Use discernment

Once you are determined to put God first, the Bible gives you something that will help you in the pursuit of a man or woman. That something is discernment.

This word means judgement, sensitivity and perception, but also one of its very interesting synonyms is 'taste'. The end of verse 2 in Romans 12 states that discerning people are able to 'taste' what is good, acceptable and perfect; they are able to act with wisdom.

Wisdom is not something we should downplay. In Proverbs, Solomon constantly encourages us to 'get wisdom' (4:5). Practically the whole books sings its praises and he tells us that wisdom is better than gold (16:16). I once heard a pastor say that wisdom is the ability to see things from God's point of view. How much do we need that in our relationships! And as followers of God, it is available to us. James tells us that if any of us lacks wisdom, let him ask God, who gives generously to all without reproach, and it will be given him (James 1:5).

This could have massive implications. Do you get accused of having poor judgement in women or men? Do you have a set taste in men or women that you will not budge on? Maybe you simply can't believe that you could pursue someone without great emphasis on physical attraction and emotion. Well, if you're really putting God first in your life, things are going to change. You'll become more discerning and you'll learn to act with wisdom, rather than foolishness.

So stop asking yourself whether you should date a suspect guy, who doesn't really love Jesus, who is trying to control you and has no job, skills or potential to provide for you. If you put God first, He'll help you discern that he is no good for you.

Stop asking yourself whether you should date a girl who's immature, conceited, flirty, a gossip, not established in character, or simply just not ready. If you put God first, you will be able discern that she is no good for you.

You see many of the main problems in dating, relationships and marriage stem from ignoring what is good, acceptable and perfect, in favour of what is ok, compromising and doubtful.

If you want a relationship that thrives, that brings God glory and that follows His design for that exciting time between single and spouse, then learn to be discerning. Surrender your desires and dreams to God, and be willing to wait for His best.

3) Do not awaken love until it's time

Sex is a gift. Like many gifts, however, if it is used wrongly or unwisely, it can lead to great pain and suffering, rather than the joy for which it was intended. Our sexuality, like all other areas of our lives, must come under God's authority if we are to receive it at its best.

God's design is that sexual intimacy be reserved for a covenant relationship, one in which a man and a woman have been united by God in marriage. It creates an environment of trust and commitment in which a man and woman give all of themselves to each other, exclusively, for life.

Now even though you may know, in your head, that God's design is perfect, you will be confronted daily with temptations that entice and cajole you to stray from what is right. In churches all across the world, God's children are being overcome by the lies of this world and are giving away the gift of their sexual purity before they are married. I have no doubt that this grieves God's heart. His very own children are rejecting His rule, and choosing a path that ultimately brings them pain and lack of fulfilment.

The Scriptures are full of warnings against compromising sexual purity, but one of the most gentle, reflecting the heart of God, is found in Song of Solomon. Again and again these words are repeated: 'I adjure you, O daughters of Jerusalem, by the gazelles or the does of the field, that you not stir up or awaken love until it pleases' (2:7).

This word *adjure* is a solemn request, an urging to grasp the importance of what is being said. With the gentleness of gazelles and does, the Lover of your soul is pleading with you not to awaken the depths of your sexual love until it is time.

This is one of God's most important commands when it comes to negotiating modern-day dating. In a world in which sex is a part of most dating relationships, God is calling you to be different, to believe His Word over the messages of the world.

As someone who has been confronted by the lies of the world so often, I can feel in myself the intensity of God's plea. Young people, older people, *anyone* who lives and breathes, listen to the Word of God on this, and do not be deceived!

Growing up in the church, many of us have been taught that sex outside of marriage is wrong, but too often we are not prepared to face the intensity of the enemy's fight to tear down our strongholds and destroy our testimonies. Be warned by the apostle Paul who says, 'Let anyone who thinks that he stands, take heed lest he fall' (1 Corinthians 10:12).

If you think that the little compromises you are making don't matter, you are deceiving yourself. The Bible says that 'among you there must not be even a hint of sexual immorality or of any kind of impurity' (Ephesians 5:3 NIV). Not even a hint! In 1 Corinthians 6:18 Christians are told to 'flee sexual immorality!' The Bible's standard for purity is not to avoid crossing the line; it's about not even getting close. And it's not just a battle of the body, but also of the mind. Jeremy Clark advises that 'to be as pure as you can be, avoid anything that awakens inappropriate desires in your mind.'[1] In the sexually saturated culture in which we live, obeying God and 'not awakening love' until it's time, calls for making radical choices in your pursuit of holiness.

As you enter a relationship with a person of the opposite sex, please listen to God's Word and His warnings. Do not believe that you are beyond temptation. Have clear boundaries that will help you hold yourself to a high standard, because your sexuality is a fire that can burn quickly out of control. It will inevitably leave in its wake the ashes of shame and regret, which are crippling the life of the church.

Many years ago an older person, who was devastated by having given up her own virginity before it was time, said to me, 'Sarah, God *must always* come first'.

Be confident, that when God comes first, you do not miss out, you thrive.

The call

Whenever we talk about dating, everyone wants the practical stuff. We're always asking that question 'What can I *do?*'

Once you're committed to putting God first and living in wisdom, there are some wise things you can do within the culture and setting in which you live, that will help you on your path to marriage.

Prepare well

One of the keys to dating well, and eventually marrying well, is to prepare well.

Maybe you're a person who is pursuing relationships, but you are simply not ready. Not ready in character, not ready in maturity, age or stage of life. Can I implore you: Don't pursue a relationship prematurely. Spend a good amount of time and prepare well; become someone who is worth dating first. That might seem a tad harsh, but some of you have not developed a character that is worth committing to; you don't have much to offer another person yet, because you haven't reinstated God's order. If that's you, don't despair. Prepare your mind, your heart and your skills.

a) Prepare your mind

> Get a correct understanding and high view of God. Knuckle down and study God's Word. Find out how to be a godly man or woman. Prepare your mind through prayer, telling God that you are willing to wait; that you're willing to lay down your sexual and sentimental priorities. Reject worldly

myths about relationships, such as the idea that you should try before you buy.

Start to think about the type of person you would like to marry and the qualities that you would hope to see in them. At the same time though, don't become dogmatic so that unless a person meets every criteria they can't be considered.

Think about who you would be prepared to date. You may be surprised who is right in front of your nose: single mums, divorcees (if Biblical circumstances allow them to remarry), people older than you and people younger than you.

Prepare your mind to be a gracious person. The truth is that these days fewer and fewer people are virgins when they marry. You should prepare your mind to be gracious to a person who has now decided to put God first in their life, but whose past will affect you. You need prepare your mind for people not to fit the mould you expected.

Prepare your mind as to how you will conduct yourself in a relationship. Before you've even met someone, you should have some definite boundaries in mind. It is helpful to have made some decisions about what you will and won't do in a relationship before you're caught up in the emotions of it all. Consider things like what your physical boundaries will be and where and when you will have alone time together. Think about some godly people in your life whom you could ask to keep you accountable and work out whether there are priorities in your life or beliefs that you're not willing to compromise on.

b) Prepare your heart

Sort out your motivations for dating. One of the biggest heart issues I see is in people who think, 'If I could just get in a relationship, all my other problems will go away'. That's a disordered motivation and it isn't true. Consider it this way: you're a sinner and the other person is a sinner, so put two sinners together and you don't get awesomeness. You get the same problems of life.

Prepare your heart to be selflessly devoted to another person. If you are locked into pornography and masturbation (which are discussed in chapters 5 and 6), you cannot be looking to a relationship as a cure. So stop pursuing one, because you are not ready. It's not fair on the other person if you begin a relationship with that kind of unresolved baggage. Learn to put God first in your life.

c) Prepare your skills

There may be some of you who really need to work on the way that you relate to the opposite sex. Being able to have meaningful conversations with someone is important. Don't carry out excessive dialogue online and then be awkward and not really speak much when you see each other. That's weird. It's counter-productive, and if you are obsessed with being online, are you really worth dating?

There are also a few gender specific things that you can really work on.

Guys: Girls don't really like it when you're overly self-conscious, when you can't string a sentence together and when your only interaction is silliness. But at the same time, they don't like over-confident loudmouths. Learn how to find the balance.

Be sincere. Learn to laugh at yourself a bit and not be too serious all the time. Ask questions about them. Focus on establishing a friendship with them, rather than coming across creepy or overbearing while you 'interview' them for the position as your wife.

Treat girls with dignity and respect. We live in a society in which women are constantly objectified and this should have no place in the church. Treat her like a lady and behave like a gentleman. This will look different for different couples because people's tastes are different, but a woman knows when she's being treated well.

Don't play games. This is one of the key ways in which people get hurt. Be prepared to be up front about your feelings and take the lead, and definitely don't string a girl along indefinitely. On the flip side though, be wise about how soon you make commitments. Don't get too serious too quickly and end up making promises that you can't keep. *

You also need to get a job, some skills and a pathway for your future. You have no right to ask for the affection of a girl if you can't sort yourself out. Here's the other thing: get an understanding of God and His Word. Godly girls will go for that. Don't just be a surface 'I love Jesus' guy; go deep in biblical wisdom and relationship with Him. Gain an understanding about what the Bible says about gender roles

---

* You may find it helpful to read our chapter on *Emotional Purity*, which will give you some insight into how women are wired for relationships.

too and what it means to be a godly leader. It is a big thing for a woman to submit herself to a man, and if you want to be worthy of that, you've got to be someone worth following.

Girls: You need to be careful about how much you let your emotions and feelings spill out unchecked. Whinging and obsessing over trivial matters tells a guy that you tend to make life about you. These things will be very unattractive to a guy.

Don't be a flirt. It's natural to enjoy being admired and noticed but be careful that your desire to feed your own needs and insecurities isn't causing you to acquire a wake of men behind you when you have no intention of getting serious.

Also, brush up on your skills in confrontation. If you know the relationship is not going anywhere, but he thinks it is, you should tell him earlier rather than later. Care for your brother in Christ. Don't lead him on because you like attention or are scared of hurting his feelings.

Don't be manipulative. Many women can really struggle in this area, and it's something you need to be conscious of when you are considering entering a relationship. Don't use your body or emotions or conversational skills to manipulate a man into giving you what you want.

One other thing that girls tend to do that can be very damaging is badmouth and gossip about Christian guys whom they personally aren't interested in. Just because you wouldn't date him, doesn't mean that someone else shouldn't. It can be very intimidating for a guy to approach a girl knowing that all the other girls will be talking about it. Pray for your friends and encourage them to seek godly men, but keep your opinions about their quirks and personalities to yourself.

Guys and girls: Make sure you develop good conversational skills. Don't go stone cold in a conversation. Give them something back. Ask them questions. Show an interest in finding out who they are and be willing to share a bit about who you are.

If you are struggling with your interactions with, and pursuit of, the opposite sex, sit down with someone you trust and ask them what you are doing wrong.

Invite someone to give you feedback and prepare yourself to hear it, even if it's tough. They may be able to tell you if you're being too overbearing, or if you look like a stone wall when someone speaks to you. People often don't really want to volunteer that information to you, but if you invite them to speak openly, you may learn some invaluable stuff.

This type of preparation will help you understand that a relationship is not about trying to get things for yourself before it's time, but about giving selflessly when you're ready. It's putting you in a place of readiness.

Date well

Dating well means becoming someone who is worthy of covenant.

That is the point of dating. You are now going from someone just worth getting to know, to someone who's actually worth making a promise to. If that's not in your headspace at all right now, then perhaps you shouldn't be dating at all.

a) Date with purpose

You should only date someone if you are seriously working towards making a promise. You need to date with purpose. You'll probably need to be discussing key things about your hopes for the future and keeping them on the agenda. At some point, you'll need to start discussing marriage.

If you are in a relationship at the moment and you're in high school, you are on a pathway which may not be wrong, but which is risky. Your relationship should be little more than a friendship and you shouldn't be having much time alone together. It should be lived out in front of family and friends. It's very difficult at that stage of life to date with marriage in mind; you just simply aren't at that stage of life. Your teenage years also give you the opportunity to build friendships and get to know different people of the opposite sex. This can be really helpful in determining what sort of person you would like to marry, and exclusive dating when you're young can hinder this.

It is important that guys are taking the lead in terms of the purpose of your relationship. If you're looking towards a biblical marriage, then young men, you need to know how to step up and be leaders.

If raising discussion about your future and marriage with the person you're with would be strange at the moment, I'd suggest there are some problems. Date with purpose. People's hearts are not something to mess around with.

b) Date with discernment

In your dating relationships, you should be asking yourself questions about the other person all along the way; not just in the initial 'tick a box' stages, but throughout the relationship.

If you constantly fight, or you find out they don't want kids, or they really feel called to be an overseas missionary and that's not you, you need to be discerning and seek the Lord.

Ending a relationship does not necessarily mean failure. Your relationships can also end whilst God's order is maintained. A dating relationship can really end in one of two ways. First, you may come to discover in your dating that God would be most glorified by you marrying that person, or second, you may discover that God would be most glorified by you not marrying that person. Either discovery is equally valid.

Though it can still hurt, the baggage is minimised when God's order has been upheld in the relationship. Be encouraged about that. The end of a relationship is not a failure in God's eyes, if God's order has been displayed.

c) Date with ministry-mindedness

Don't disappear when you get into a relationship. The church still wants to see you. Your family wants to see you and one of the best ways you will affirm your relationship before God is by actively serving him in the church together.

So be around. Get serving together. Excessive privacy is a killer of relationships, so date with ministry mindedness—that's healthy.

Relationships are not one-size-fits-all. They are unique, because people are unique. But that's the beauty of God's order. It is one-size-fits-all. If you are determined to put God first, if you're discerning about who you're pursuing, and if you're preparing yourself to be someone worthy of covenant, then you can be sure that, by God's leading and empowerment, you will be able to date well.

If your dating is focused on glorifying God, and you're dating with purpose, discernment and ministry mindedness, you can once again be confident of God's leading. And if you date well, you will be prepared to marry well.

CHAPTER 2

Singleness: Embracing God's will for 'now'

Sarah Rose

Kylie walked across the darkened car park, shivering slightly from the chill after the warmth of indoors. A subtle smile was still plastered on her face, as though it had become stuck there after wearing it all day. As she reached her car and climbed in, the silence enveloped her, more noticeable after the lively conversation and upbeat music inside.

She turned on the engine, noting the green glow of the clock saying 11:56. As she maneuvered out of the car park Kylie squirmed, adjusting her dress and pivoting her high heels to work with the clutch and the brake. The sense of elegance she'd felt inside faded as she drove herself through the night. It had been a great night, but despite the hours of laughter and dancing and good food, she suddenly felt like she was all dressed up with nowhere to go.

She'd always loved weddings, but she was starting to lose track of how many she'd been to. How many nights like this had she driven home alone, while another good friend, this time six years younger than her, drove away with her new husband?

The silence of the car and the constancy of the streetlights, cold and amber as they flashed past, brought her back to the harsh reality. The fairy-tale she'd always imagined had turned out to be just that. Not real. A figment of her childhood imagination.

She'd always imagined that romance, love and marriage were just a part of life; that they happened to everyone. Now she was wondering if it was something that just happened to other people. She wondered how she'd become caught on the outside, always looking in.

By the time she reached home, the magic of the day had disappeared. She let herself into the dark house and walked to her bedroom. As she turned on the lamp she caught sight of herself in the mirror. She straightened and looked at the figure staring back at her. The elegant dress, the carefully curled hair, the meticulously applied makeup, the high-heeled shoes. All of it was designed to make her look her best. And it worked. In the glow of the lamplight, she looked beautiful, but with that recognition came an emptiness. What was the point when there was no one to appreciate it?

Kylie washed off her make-up, undressed and put on her pyjamas. She climbed into bed alone and switched off the light. As she lay in the darkness she felt the unbidden stinging behind her eyes. She squeezed them tightly shut, but still, the silent tears leaked out.

The culture

If you're single, long after you'd hoped to be married, you will know the pain of being alone. You know what it's like to be home alone on a Friday night, or to have no one to take to that work dinner. You know what it's like to see friends happily married and having children, so that you no longer fit into their lives in the way that you used to. You know what it's like to wonder how you missed out, when it seems to work for everyone else. You've been asked the question, over and over again 'Why aren't you married?' and you laugh it off and give some kind of trite answer, all the while agonizing over it in your own heart. Because as single people, we desperately want an answer to that question. In fact, a lot of our self-worth can be caught up in that question, because we all know that there is one answer, niggling beneath the surface that we can neither face nor escape: What if I'm not married because nobody wants me?

I (Sarah) know that single life can often feel like a waiting game. And then you realize that meeting your match just might not happen, and you have to wonder, is there more to life than this?

If you're a single person, chances are you're tired of the struggle; tired of wondering why it is that dozens of people around you have found 'the one' while you're still alone; tired of feeling like you're on the outside looking in, and tired of wondering what you're supposed to do with your life until you finally find your match and everything can 'get back on course'.

This chapter is for you, and it's not about waiting. It's about living abundantly, because that's what God intended. It's about discovering that there *is* more to life and that God has a plan for you that is not second best. It's about finding hope and joy and loving life despite your relationship status.

The Scripture

One of the great secrets to living an abundant life and pleasing God is contentment. Contentment isn't just patient resignation; it's actually an ability to find joyful satisfaction despite our circumstances. In Philippians 4, Paul said that he had learned to be content in whatever situation he was in (v11), and he'd faced some pretty tough situations.

Is it possible that you struggle intensely with being single because you haven't yet learned to rejoice in what God has for you now? Are you constantly looking forward, desperately hoping for better circumstances?

In order to be content with where God has placed you, you need to understand His heart on this issue. You need to understand that God is not giving you second best, and that He has not forgotten you. You need to discover the gift that He has for you in your singleness.

Singleness is not second best

The idol of marriage

Church culture tends to idolize marriage. I'm sure that you, like me, often find that one of the most challenging things about being single is watching the way in which people who manage to 'overcome' their singleness are celebrated. It seems to be a self-appointed role of many married people, to do what they can to 'fix' a single person's state by finding them a partner. When two people succeed in starting a relationship, people rejoice and news flies quickly. When people become engaged we celebrate again. They have a big party and people bring presents to help the couple set up their new home. And it doesn't stop there. At kitchen teas, hens and bucks nights and the wedding itself, the happy couple and their love is celebrated and they are showered with gifts and cash. Single people often spend these events being asked when they're going to find someone (as if we know the answer to that question!) and when it's all over they go back to work on Monday to save up some money to set up their own homes, by themselves.

We should absolutely celebrate marriage, but it is important to realize, with a culture like this, that it is no wonder that single people can feel like they're getting second best. Not only are they alone, but no one is celebrating them. Single life isn't seen as much to be celebrated.

A high view of singleness

The Bible, however, does not conform to the world's views on singleness. In fact, it has a very high view of what it is to be single. Have you ever really stopped to think about the fact that the two people who had the absolute greatest impact throughout the entirety of the New Testament were both single? Jesus and Paul were hardly men that you'd say God had forgotten about, nor were they men that God was giving second best to, and they both spoke about singleness.

It can be encouraging to realize that, though they lived in a culture in which marriage was even more the norm than it is in ours, Paul and Jesus both presented singleness as a legitimate and highly valuable state.

In 1 Corinthians 7, Paul talks in detail about both marriage and singleness. In fact Paul said to the unmarried and the widows that 'it is good for them to remain single as I am' (1 Corinthians 7:8). This was astonishing in a time in which marriage and family was not only a source of pride, but also of security. But culture had changed for the early church. Family was no longer purely defined by genetics, but by rebirth into the kingdom of God. The church no longer relied purely on their immediate families to care for them, but they cared willingly for each other. Instead of finding themselves in situations where they had to marry, widows or young people were free, through the support of the church, to serve God in a greater capacity. As Keller writes, 'Christians who remained single, then, were making the statement that our future is not guaranteed by the family but by God.'[1] For perhaps the first time in history, and quite counter-culturally, singleness was a viable and celebrated option. Paul even said that because the time was short those who had wives were to 'live as though they had none' (1 Corinthians 7:29). The Kingdom was at hand, there was work to do, and single people, who had their eyes firmly fixed on Jesus, could play a unique role.

But my life feels incomplete!

The idol of 'the one'

I don't know about you, but one of the things I've really wrestled with, as a single person, is the sense of just not feeling complete. We live in a world that is seemingly made for pairs. People talk about meeting their 'perfect match', their 'other half' and their 'soul mate'. Decades worth of songs have crooned that 'you're nobody, 'till somebody loves you'[2] and that 'I have nothing… if I don't have you'.[3]

Our culture may not hold marriage very highly, but it practically worships sex. It may not care if you're single, but it has a low tolerance for celibacy, and we single Christians know it. Not only is the concept of sexual purity daunting enough in itself for the single Christian wanting to live God's way, but it comes with the knowledge that the world around us mocks it and even considers it shameful. Not only that, but in the words of Lina Abujamra: 'We live in a culture that idolizes the "big love" so much so that it's hard for any of us to understand how anyone can choose anything over true love'.[4]

God, the one and only

Despite the fact that the world often offers human relationships as the means by which the deepest desires of our hearts can be met, over and over people are discovering that they can be as lonely and unfulfilled within a relationship as they can be out of it.

Augustine famously quoted 'Thou hast made us for thyself and restless is our heart until it comes to rest in Thee'.[5] Anyone who is looking to a marriage partner to fulfil their deepest needs and desires will be disappointed. Married people were never designed to find their completeness in their spouse, and single people were never designed to find their completion in marriage.

God made us for community with others, but he primarily made our souls to find their deepest satisfaction and fulfilment in Him. King David, who was surrounded by people and had several wives, consistently looked to God to fulfil his deepest needs. In Psalm 73 he says 'whom have I in heaven but you? And there is nothing on earth that I desire besides you... God is the strength of my heart and my portion forever' (v25-26).

If David can say these things, how much more can we, as the church of Jesus Christ, say them? Colossians 2 tells us that in Jesus the 'whole fullness of deity dwells bodily, and you have been filled in Him, who is the head of all rule and authority' (2:9-10). As Christians we are indwelt by the Spirit of God himself and He is committed to transforming us into the likeness of Jesus Christ so that we may be 'perfect and complete, lacking in nothing' (James 1:4).

Singleness, rather than being a state of incompletion, affords us the opportunity to discover the source of our true completion. While God calls many to be married, He does not call anyone to find their identity or security in anyone beside Himself.

Sometimes I've found myself feeling like Jesus is the consolation prize; the 'back up husband' that I get because I haven't found a real one, but God is teaching me that nothing could be further from the truth. Jesus is more of a companion, provider, leader, comforter and sacrificial lover than any husband or wife could ever be. Being single can force a person to deepen their trust and relationship with Jesus because they don't have the distraction of a spouse that gives the allusion of providing those things. Getting to know Jesus, as the bridegroom on earth is not a disadvantage, but a privilege, and one that leads to a radical and fulfilling life.

Singleness: The gift I never wanted

What do we do with the single Christian?

Even once we recognize that God sees great value in singleness, the concept of 'the gift of singleness' is a tough one to grasp. For many of us, it's the gift we never wanted and we can relate to Lina Abujamra's quip that 'If singleness is a gift, can someone please point me to the returns counter?'[6]

Well meaning, married Christians have long used this 'gift' concept to reconcile in themselves the dilemma of this rare and somewhat foreign species: the single Christian.

'Oh, you're not married?' they say with surprise, looking somewhat confused and worried, until it clicks for them.

'Well, you must have the gift of singleness!' they say with triumph, as if having managed to solve your 'problem'.

When they say 'gift of singleness' this is what they mean: A state in which God has called and equipped you to live the single life without feeling the need to get married or the strong drive towards sexual intimacy.

The problem with this concept is that there are a growing number of single people in the church who would very much like to be married, who don't feel uniquely gifted to be single or celibate, and who are confused about whether or not they have this (very undesirable) gift. This can leave us with a number of questions:

If I desire to get married, does that mean I will get married? If I don't have the gift of singleness, why am I not married? Is singleness a gift that can be chosen, or is it given?

What did Jesus and Paul mean by the 'gift of singleness?'

Learning to be thankful

In Matthew 19, Jesus said to his disciples:

> Not everyone can receive this saying, but only those to whom it is given. For there are eunuchs who have been so from birth, and there are eunuchs who have been made eunuchs by men, and there are eunuchs who have made themselves eunuchs for the sake of the kingdom of heaven. Let the one who is able to receive this receive it.(v11-12)

When confronted with Jesus' high view of marriage, the disciples wondered whether a person might find it better just not to marry at all. Jesus validated this as a reasonable choice, though he made it clear that it wasn't for everyone. He said that 'not everyone can receive [it] but only those to whom it has been given'. He then went on to speak of eunuchs, something common in their day, but quite uncommon for us. These were men who had been castrated and therefore felt no desire or need for sexual intimacy. Jesus said 'there are eunuchs who have made themselves eunuchs for the sake of the Kingdom of heaven. Let the one who is able to receive this receive it'.

Jesus was not advocating literal castration here, but was speaking figuratively of those who, looking at the needs and ministry opportunities around them, make a choice to sacrifice the intimacy of a marriage relationship and remain celibate so that they could best be used for the kingdom. These people have been specifically gifted by God to receive this gift that not only enables them to be single and chaste, but also to desire it. You could say that these people have been gifted *for* singleness.

The apostle Paul appears to have been one of these people. He could see the benefits of being single and he chose it for the sake of the Kingdom. This can be rather hard for some of us to understand. As Elisabeth Elliot jokingly quipped, '[Paul] was single because he liked being single and I was suspicious of a man like that'.[7] I can certainly relate! I mean, good for Paul if he enjoyed it, but the vast majority of single Christians in the modern western church are not single because we have desired or chosen it; we have trouble seeing it as a gift. What does the Bible say to us?

While Jesus' words seem specifically targeted to those choosing a life of singleness, Paul's words are actually a bit broader. In fact, he says that 'each has his [or her] own gift from God, one of one kind and one of another' (1 Corinthians 7:7). Paul is saying that every person *has* a gift, either of marriage or of singleness. He does not say *will one day have*, but rather, present tense, *has*. Whatever your current state, it is a gift from God that comes with its own unique enabling and 'perks'. If you are single now, then you currently have the gift that is singleness. You may not have been gifted *for* singleness, but you have been gifted *with* it. Too many single people get so caught up with whether or not they have been specifically gifted (against their will!) for lifelong singleness that they fail to recognize that their current state of singleness is a gift.

If you feel like singleness is the gift you never wanted, take a moment to remember that there is more to a gift than the gift itself. There is also a giver. In this case the giver is the God of the universe who knows you better than you know yourself. Sometimes the things God gives us in this life don't look too appealing, but more often than not, the things that we never would have chosen for ourselves, turn out to be the greatest blessings.

I can testify to this in my own life. I had a plan. I was going to be married at 22. It seemed like a good age, and, I wanted to be a young mum. If I'd known as an 18 year old that not only was I not going to be married by 22, but that by 28 I still would not be married, and would possibly *never* marry, my small world would have fallen apart. But now, as I look back, I do not for one second regret that I was not married at 22. I can see that being single during those years was truly a gift, albeit one that I didn't want, and it enabled me to do and achieve things both in my personal life and in my ministry that I would otherwise not have done. Now, as I look to the future, I have to believe that if I am to remain single, that too will be a gift.

God has gifted and called us all to different things at different times of our lives for the sake of His glorious work. We must never fail to remember that He is not only the one who calls, but also the one who gives the grace, enablement and provision to carry out what He calls us to do.

Take a moment to thank God for the gifts He has given you, and ask him to show you how your singleness can be a gift to you and others at this point in your life.

The call

As young people living in a world that seems to have its identity tied up in a tangled web of marriage, sexuality, independence and relationships, it is so important that you, as a part of the church, are demonstrating accurately who you are in Christ. Our culture desperately needs people who are secure in their identity, who are not consumed with changing their marital statuses and who are able to work with freedom and joy in the ministry in which God has placed them.

Surrender

One thing that you are called to do as a Christian is to present your body as a living sacrifice, holy and pleasing to God (Romans 12:1). This act of surrender means laying your dreams and desires on the altar before God, and allowing Him to have free reign in your life. Part of this involves coming to terms with the fact that marriage is not a right. Just because it is the norm, and just because it is a good thing, does not mean God owes it to you.

The desire to get married and have a family is not wrong. Asking God to give it to you is not wrong. What is wrong is when that desire becomes so much of a consuming priority that you are unwilling to surrender it to the will of God. If you are in love with the idea of marriage, more than you are in love with God, it has become an idol, and idols have no place in the heart of one of God's children.

Keller stresses that:

> We should be neither overly elated by getting married nor overly disappointed by not being so—because Christ is the

only spouse that can truly fulfil us and God's family the only family that will truly embrace and satisfy us.[8]

Surrendering means trusting that God's ways are higher than your ways and placing yourself on the altar to be used for His purposes above your own. It also means not comparing yourself to others. God does not have the same plan for all of us. He will require things of you that He may not ask of others. Comparison breeds jealousy and bitterness, and stops you from flourishing in the way that God intends.

Trust in the goodness of God

Do you really believe that God can be trusted with your life?

In order to really thrive as a single person, it is imperative that your view of God is not flawed. Remember, your vision is very limited. You see your life here on earth, and it can seem so long; so complete. What you may often forget is that God sees the whole picture, and the whole picture is infinitely bigger than you realize. Do you realize that your life here on earth is just a tiny blip on the scale of your whole existence? You were made for eternity!

Remember that God sees the end from the beginning and that His ways are higher than yours (Isaiah 55:9), that He has loved you with an everlasting love (Psalm 103:17) and that He works all things together for your good (Romans 8:28).

This God who created you for relationship with Himself, is not out to cause you pain! Jesus experienced agonizing pain for the sake of redeeming you. He didn't do that, only to decide that He doesn't care that much about you after all.

Psalm 9:10 says that 'those who know Your name put their trust in You'. If you truly know God, you will trust Him, because He is completely trustworthy. If you are struggling to trust God with your singleness, the solution is to get to know Him more. Read about Him, seek His promises, pray through your feelings, ask Him to help you surrender, and trust that if He has called you to something difficult, His reasoning and his outcomes will be amazingly worth it!

Find the community God has for you

While you were made to be complete in Christ, you were not made to be alone. God created you for community and He created men and women to complement each other. For the most part, this is exhibited through marriage and family, but it is equally important in your life as a single person.

The world is plagued by the consequences of ungodly relationships, and it can be tempting to throw up your hands in defeat and claim loudly, 'I don't need anyone!' It is important as you learn to embrace the value of singleness, not to reject the importance and beauty of community and relationship. Married people need to ensure that single people are welcomed into their lives, and as a single person you need to be involved in deep spiritual friendships. Churches also need to work on ways in which both genders can work in a complementary way, whether married or single. Men were not made to relate solely to men, nor women to women, but both genders are to work together for the glory of God.

Have a think about which people in your own life God wants you to build spiritual community with. Who are they and how can you develop a sense of family?

It is also important that you don't become so consumed with your independence and autonomy that you lose the value of marriage. I know personally that this can be tempting when you're coming to terms with the fact that you may not marry. In order to make yourself feel better you can focus on the negatives of marriage and over-glorify singleness, in particular the freedom it seems to afford us to live more independent (and often selfish!) lives. While it is important that you embrace God's calling on your life while you are single, it is also important that you don't reject the idea of marriage. Marriage is a noble pursuit, but it is never to be your main pursuit.

Embrace the gift

If you have a supremely high view of the gospel of Jesus Christ, you will discover something exciting: you have been uniquely gifted for the work of God on earth, just through your singleness!

Relationships take time and care, and God knows this, but you can almost sense Paul's excitement as he reminds single people that there are certain roles and distractions that they don't have in their lives. You can almost see his eyes shining as he looks at the single person and says 'look how much undivided devotion you can give to the Lord!'

Don't fall into the trap of putting your life on hold, waiting for marriage. There is a lot you can actively embrace about this gift of being single. Marshall Segal puts it well when he says:

> A season of singleness is not merely the minor leagues of marriage. It has the potential to be a unique period of undivided devotion to Christ and undistracted ministry to others. With the Spirit in you and the calendar clear, God

has given you the means to make a lasting difference for his kingdom. You're all dressed up, having every spiritual blessing in the heavenly places (Ephesians 1:3), with literally everywhere to go.[9]

Do not keep the gift to yourself! You may not have a life partner, but you have still been made and uniquely gifted for community. Use your singleness to serve others. Your ability to invest time in those outside your own family is much greater than those who have to focus on raising a family. You have the opportunity to pour godly influence into a range of different lives. You are much more able to go at the drop of a hat, invest time in prayer, and travel to places that others find it difficult to go. Can I encourage you, as I must often encourage myself, to use the gift of singleness for the building up of the church, rather than for selfish pursuits? It is so easy to fall into the trap of feeling like your singleness has somehow earned you the right to live a pleasure-filled, self-focused life. Single people often have more money, more time and more freedom than those who have families. Instead of seeing it as an opportunity to consume earthly pleasures and experiences, see it as an opportunity to invest more in God's kingdom.

Choose to enjoy your singleness and the unique opportunities it affords. It may not last forever, and if it does, God will give you the grace each day to deal with it. When God calls you to be single for a time, He is not giving you second best. He knows that singleness is often painful. He knows what it is to be alone, but He also knows this: That there is a joy to be found in Him and a purpose in His work that can fulfil you in a way that no earthly relationship could. So, precious single person, turn your eyes to Him and pursue Him above all other relationships, and see if He does not fill you with joy and contentment that you'd never thought were possible.

CHAPTER 3

Emotional purity: Guarding your heart and your emotions

Sarah Rose

Long after church had ended, a young man and woman sat in a car in the darkness and seclusion of the church car park. Everyone else had left. Their friendship was at an impasse; they both knew it couldn't turn into a romantic relationship, but it was so hard to let go! The intimacy they had built over weeks of deep conversations and long late-night phone calls left them with few options. Begin an official relationship that neither of them really wanted, or end the intimate nature of the friendship, which probably meant ending the friendship altogether. As the hours ticked by in the darkness, they gorged themselves on their final forbidden meal of emotional intimacy, sharing secrets that they never intended to share. Finally, in the early hours of the morning, they left in their separate cars. They'd never even touched each other, but when the woman woke up the next morning, she felt the sickness of regret; the dirtiness that came with emotional promiscuity.

The culture

We tend to emphasise the physical side of purity, but have you ever stopped to think that there could be a lot more to it than that? Issues of purity begin in our hearts and can very quickly, and often undetected, make their way into our minds, sentiments and emotions.

The story above may seem strange to you and you may even think it sounds a bit extreme, but I can say on behalf of thousands of women, and some men too, that the pain and complexity of misplaced emotional intimacy is very real.

It's something that's very close to my heart, because I've struggled with it for most of my life. What made matters worse was that I didn't even realize that the problem existed until half way through my twenties when I read Shannon Ethridge's book *Every Woman's Battle*.

Church culture often implies that as long as a couple has boundaries in place and are keeping themselves physically pure they will not compromise their integrity. This concept is dangerously flawed and demonstrates a fundamental misunderstanding of the way in which men and women are wired.

So, what do I mean when I talk about emotional purity? I'm talking about issues of lust that don't centre primarily on the physical, but rather the mind and the emotions. I'm talking about fantasizing. I'm talking about consuming emotional porn and I'm talking about pursuing deep relational connections with the opposite sex without real commitment for the purpose of lustful fulfilment.

Heavy stuff hey? It is, but it's also very real.

There are four areas in which emotional purity has become an issue in the church:

1) The plight of women in the battle for sexual purity has largely been overlooked. You may have grown up thinking of this as a man's battle, but did you realize that women struggle just as much? While a man's battle with lust often centres on what he sees and experiences physically, a woman's battle centres around what she hears and experiences emotionally. Women crave deeply intimate emotional relationships in a similar way to which men crave intimate physical relationships and they will often compromise their integrity in order to fill this craving.

2) Women often struggle with counterfeit emotional fantasies in a similar way to which men struggle with counterfeit physical fantasies. The fact that the porn industry is aimed predominantly at men may have led you to believe that men are the ones who struggle with sexual sin. But have you ever noticed that entire industries are aimed at engaging women's emotional fantasies? Both the film and book industries have long made money from women's desires to fill themselves with what can, in extreme cases, be labelled as emotional porn. While a man may struggle with being glued to the fantasies inside his computer screen, women have long been curled up in a corner with a book or movie that excites them with its romantic dialogue and ever emotionally available heroes.

3) Many women caught up in this can testify to the dangerous combination of their unique struggle for sexual

purity with the wide acceptance of emotionally intimate relationships. While an emotionally close relationship with a girlfriend or girl friend may be a pleasant and enjoyable experience for a man, it is often a far deeper experience for a woman. Not only does she enjoy the experience, but every conversation leaves her wanting to go deeper, desiring to capture more of a man's heart and soul.

4) Many young people are sharing the deepest parts of their souls with each other, without the security of any kind of commitment. Close friendship and deep conversation build intimacy and many young men and women are enjoying a level of intimacy outside of marriage, or even outside of a dating relationship, that develops ties and connections that they have no intention of maintaining long term.

Can you see how this could affect the church? Countless young adults are suffering in broken relationships and counterfeit fantasies that are sapping their time and energy. They are able to offer little hope to a world reeling from the effects of broken hearts, divorce and separation. And therein lies the greatest tragedy. When we compromise on any area of our sexuality, emotional intimacy included, we end up tangled in a web of brokenness, unable to offer the hope, love and joy of Jesus to others so desperately in need.

I'd encourage you to examine your own heart in this area, as we delve into what the Bible has to say about emotional purity.

The Scripture

God's design for intimacy

Do you realize that God has designed you with powerful potential for intimacy? The word 'intimacy' denotes a sense of closeness, familiarity, affection for or deep knowledge of something. Humans, more than any other part of His creation, have both the potential and desire to cultivate intimate relationships.

Many people experience some level of closeness with each other, but very early in Genesis, God reveals the pinnacle of human intimacy: the union between a man and a woman. In Genesis 2, we see that God's design for marriage is 'a man shall leave his father and his mother and hold fast to his wife, and they shall become one flesh' (2:24). Jesus confirms this in Mark 10 saying '...they are no longer two but one flesh. What therefore God has joined together let no man separate' (10:8-9). Here we see a picture that goes far beyond a white dress and exchange of rings. We see God actively uniting two people to such an extent that they become one. It's interesting that the word 'flesh' is included in both of these verses. In Hebrew and Greek, 'flesh' refers both to the body and the living human in general. Not only were Adam and Eve joined physically through sexual intercourse, but they were also joined intimately in their daily lives and purpose on the earth. Eve was created as an 'ezer' or 'helper' for Adam. She was a partner not only in body, but also in life. Their nakedness before each other was complete, both physically and emotionally.

God designed intimacy between a husband and wife not only to be deep and complete but also exclusive. The joining of two people in intimate union is something God has reserved for a committed and covenant relationship. The Scripture warns over and over against behaviour that ruins one's entry into this covenant of intimacy. This behaviour includes fornication, which is the pre-marital sexual union of two people, but this physical action is not the only behaviour that the Scriptures warn against. Song of Solomon, in the midst of its celebration of the intimate love between and man and woman, implores its readers not to 'stir up or awaken love until it pleases' (2:7). In a similar way, Proverbs 4 tells us to 'above all else, guard your heart, for everything you do flows from it' (v23 NIV).

Each of these verses pre-empt the fact that as humans, we will desire a level of intimacy that is reserved for the covenant relationship of marriage, before the commitment is made. God is concerned not only that you keep the *act* of sexual intercourse for marriage, but also that you are guarded in other ways. The heart, being the wellspring of life, is the source of not only your desires and feelings, but the very essence of who you are. It is no wonder that it should be guarded.

So what about close friendships? Well, God not only affirms, but encourages deep spiritual friendship. As we search the Scriptures though, we find that outside of the marriage covenant it is almost exclusively with people of the same gender. David and Jonathan are the classic example. First Samuel tells us that Jonathan loved David 'as he loved his own soul' (20:17). No godly friendship is condemned in Scripture, but as a discerning Christian you need to recognize the fundamental difference in God's design for relationship between persons of the same gender and persons of the opposite sex.

Men and women have been created to bond together with an intimacy far beyond that of any other relationship. A friendship between a male and a female has the potential to ignite a love and passion that can quickly burn out of control, because they were made to fit together in a divinely intimate way. Same gender friends are able to enjoy a deep level of friendship without the fear of finding themselves too intimately connected.[†]

As you reflect on this, it might be helpful for you to have a think about your own friendships and your motives behind them. Is it possible that you have cultivated a level of intimacy with someone of the opposite sex that is not in line with your level of commitment? If so, what do you think God would have you do about it?

Eve's battle

While God has made both men and women with a desire for intimacy with each other, He has also made them *differently*. You've probably heard it said that 'men give love to get sex, and women give sex to get love'. Sure, it's a broad generalisation, but it highlights the fact that in general men crave physical intimacy, while women crave emotional intimacy.

The above saying has been used in church and general culture to warn women against giving away their bodies to men in the hope of receiving emotional love in return. The church seems to have made men's fallen nature the enemy of sexual purity, and it is as though no one stopped to wonder if maybe it was a two way street. The words 'love' and 'sex' in this saying have overshadowed the core of the problem, which is evidenced in the words 'give to get'. Far from God's original design which could

---

[†] *(NB: As a result of the fall, God's perfect design is not always evident. Sometimes same gender relationships can become too passionate and burn out of control. If you are struggling with same gender attraction, have a look at our chapter on homosexuality.)*

be described better as 'give to serve,' the battle for sexuality has become all about what we can get. Both men and women are equally prone to manipulation and compromise in order to fulfil their selfish desires.

These selfish desires mean that not only do we attempt to 'awaken love before it pleases' but we step far away from God's design in order to do so. Women, with their unique wiring, tend to be tempted to do this in their search for emotional intimacy.

The fall has given birth to three things in the heart of a woman that compromise her emotional purity: the desire to control, possess and manipulate; an inclination towards idolatry; and the lust of the heart.

1) The desire to control, possess and manipulate

In Genesis 3, after Eve ate the forbidden fruit, God outlined some gender specific struggles that both Adam and Eve would face as a result of their sin. Eve was first told that she would have pain in childbirth (v16) (yep, we all see that one playing out) but then she was told something that is somewhat more subtle and mysterious. God told Eve 'Your desire shall be for your husband, and he shall rule over you' (v16). This can be a challenging verse but commentators seem to be fairly united in their understanding of it. Köstenberger puts it like this: 'As far as the woman's relationship with her husband is concerned, loving harmony will be replaced by a pattern in which the woman seeks to exert control over her husband...'[1]

In the same way that Eve's pain in childbirth has been passed on to her daughters, so has this desire for control. A woman's healthy desire for emotional intimacy can easily become a power issue. While men may gain a sense of power from a sexual 'conquest,' women feel powerful if they can 'conquer' a man emotionally. When you start looking for it, you may be surprised by the extent to which this is evident in reality. Just take a look at films that are marketed predominantly towards women. The majority of male protagonists fall into one of two categories: the somewhat weak and flawed, but absolutely lovable, Hugh Grant type; or the rebellious bad-boy Johnny Depp type who, somewhere deep inside, has a good heart. Why is it that these rather opposite types appeal to women so much? Partly, because it feeds their desire for power. A passive man makes a woman feel powerful through his weakness and his need for her to lead and even mother him. The bad-boy can create a desire in a woman to save him. If she can tame him, or redeem him, she feels within herself both powerful and worthwhile.

Unfortunately the world we live in has long associated power and authority with worth. Women can become jaded by this view and hold to the belief that in order to be valuable, they must be powerful. Because men have historically held the balance of power, a woman feels that if she can gain control over a man, she has proven herself to be someone of worth.

The desire to make a man subject to her can run deep within the sinful heart of a woman. As Christian women we must let our hearts be informed by the truth of the Gospel. We must find our worth in God's impartial love that does not see value in terms of rank, or gender, or gifting or authority.

Having a Biblically informed understanding of where your faults and weaknesses lie can be one of the keys to cultivating a heart that pursues emotional purity.

2) An inclination towards idolatry

Instead of focusing our hearts and minds on our Creator, we as women, often allow ourselves to become consumed with the quest for earthly relationships. We are prone to idolise the concepts of marriage, emotional intimacy and romance. Sometimes we can spend hours planning and, let's face it, plotting ways in which our emotional cravings can be met.

How much time do you spend dreaming about relationships? How often do you find yourself looking at wedding dresses, or planning your big day, or naming your children, or dreaming about romantic scenarios? Those things in and of themselves are not wrong but they can quickly escalate out of control.

The Bible teaches us that we are to have one consuming passion in our lives: that we are to love the Lord our God with all our heart, soul, mind and strength (Mark 12:30). It also tells us in Colossians 3:5 that we are to put to death earthly passions, evil desires and covetousness, which is idolatry.

Throughout the Bible there are countless stories of people whose downfall came because they valued something or someone more than God. If there are things in your life that you are desiring, coveting or pursuing in an obsessive way, so that they are becoming idols, ask God to help you put them back in their rightful place.

3) *The lust of the heart*

The Bible has a lot to say about lust, but I fear that far too often the women switch off because they don't struggle so much with the lust of the eyes. If, however, God desires us not only be physically pure but emotionally pure too, women very quickly find themselves back in the game. When we think of lust, we often think of a man looking at a woman with the desire to have sex with her. But what makes lust wrong? Lust is wrong when it is a consuming desire to have something that is not yours. Its covetous and controlling nature makes it not only sinful, but also a form of idolatry.

Lust is a very serious issue, made even more serious because it is often overlooked in the hearts of women. One of the passages most commonly used to convict men about lust is in Matthew 5, which says '...anyone who looks at a woman lustfully has already committed adultery with her in his heart' (v28). While a *man's* eyes are the vehicles for the main issue of lust here, the point that Jesus is trying to make is that if you allow a sinful desire to take root in your heart, then as far as your heart is concerned, the sin is committed.

I know many guys who are disgusted by the way in which young Christian women perv on male celebrities, raving about how gorgeous or hot or dreamy they are. This is the kind of behaviour that women wouldn't tolerate in Christian men and yet somehow they let themselves off the hook.

Even if you are not someone who engages in *looking* at men to lust after them, how often do you dwell on things that they say? You may not fantasize so much about physical intimacy, but how often do you fantasize about emotional intimacy?

You may not look at images of naked men, but how often do you put yourself mentally in the place of the heroine in a novel or movie, imagining that the words the hero is saying to her are being said to you?

For women, the emotional is very closely linked with the sexual. Any emotional fantasies you have about a man who is not your husband are very often also sexual fantasies, even if they don't actually involve the sexual act. When you search the Scriptures to see what it says about lust, there is no way that you can separate yourself from its teaching as though it is not your issue.

God wants so much more for His daughters than unsatisfying lusts of the heart that lead to emotional promiscuity and counterfeit relationships. He desires to fill you with Himself and restore you so that you can give yourself to *one* man within the safety of a covenant relationship.

The call

Do not awaken love

The desire for sexual and emotional intimacy can be very strong, especially in a culture that flaunts and encourages it. God is calling you to a high standard, not to limit you, but because you were created for something greater. The wise man and woman do not put themselves in positions where the strong, burning desire for something that they cannot have is prematurely awakened. Don't believe the world's lie that suppressing your desires is harmful. God wants you to bring your desires before Him, and then trust Him with them by exercising self-control over them.

It is also important that you are not deceived about the power of emotional connection. Because the emotional is so closely linked to the sexual, emotional compromise can lead both to physical compromise and to pornography and masturbation.

The battle of emotional lust does not magically cease when you find someone to marry. In fact, one of our church counsellors has made this observation:

> It seems to me that emotional intimacy is the number one reason for affairs and/or discontentment in marriage… in our experience all affairs or discontentment have begun with long conversations, even 'spiritual' ones, with someone of the opposite sex.

A lax attitude to emotional promiscuity is not something you want to take into marriage with you, so it is important to start working out boundaries and strategies now.

Today's technology makes it easier than ever to become emotionally attached to another person with little real-life commitment. Be prepared to make wise decisions about how you use your phone or computer to communicate. Messaging that moves into how you feel about things opens the door to emotional connection. Several years ago God convicted me about how emotionally involved I could get with people online. I took the step to remove the 'instant chat' option from my computer, and began the process of disconnecting myself from deeply conversational relationships that weren't going anywhere in the long term, but were gratifying my short term desires. Have a think about how you use technology and whether this may be an area of emotional compromise for you.

Determine to be a woman of emotional purity

Women, like all Christians, you are called to renounce idolatry. Perhaps it is time for you to examine your life (as I often have to do with mine) to see what you are holding onto too tightly. Maybe it's a relationship with a man that you can't have, either because he is married, unsaved or unsuited to you. Perhaps it's a stash of romantic books or movies, or perhaps it is a consuming desire to get married that finds you searching the internet for pictures of dresses, rings and dream honeymoon destinations. If you want to be a woman of high emotional integrity, don't be surprised if God starts talking to you about things in your life that you are holding too close. Remember that your life is not your own and that you were bought with a price. God deserves and desires all of you and He has the right to supremacy in every place in your heart.

As you determine in your heart to be a woman of emotional purity, it may be helpful to ask yourself the following questions:

- Is there a man (or men) in my life from whom I receive a level of emotional or sexual gratification that does not match our mutual level of commitment to each other?
- Am I feeding my lusts for emotional intimacy with counterfeit men or scenarios in books or movies?
- Am I seeking to manipulate, control or possess power over a man by what I wear, what I say, or how I act?
- Am I guarding my heart and not giving away too much of myself to a man, even if I think he may be a potential husband?
- If I am married, am I entertaining thoughts about other men, whether real or imagined, that are not helpful or honouring towards my husband?

These questions are difficult. Women, I feel your pain as I have, over the years, slowly begun to extract from my own life elements of emotional compromise that operated undetected for years. But we are called to something greater. We are called not to conform to the pattern of this world, but to be transformed by the renewing of our minds (Romans 12:2). The secret to renewing our minds can be found in 2 Corinthians where we are commended to 'take every thought captive to obey Christ' (10:5). Once you have determined to be a woman of emotional purity, and once you have identified your weak areas, it is important that you guard your mind and your heart by taking control over your thoughts. A thought can develop into a lustful fantasy in less than a second, and when this happens, you must be quick to capture it and make it subject to the call and will of Christ.

Such a task is too great for you alone, but praise God for the Holy Spirit who gives you strength when you are weak. You can be confident that those things that God calls you to do, He also strengthens you to do. God calls you to do only that which is for your ultimate good. You may also find it beneficial to enlist the help of a trusted friend or mentor to hold you accountable as you determine to be a woman who is pure in her emotions and sentiments.

Pursue Christ

The process of removing inappropriate emotional relationships or fantasies from your life can leave you with times of loneliness and emptiness that can be a breeding ground for temptation. One of our church's counsellors, Kerri, shared:

> For me, a vital component in liberating myself is to replace my sinful feelings with an intimate love for Jesus. Experiencing

intimacy with Him over time removes the strength of the bind I can have with the wrong person, and is ultimately satisfying.

Instead of focusing on avoiding the wrong behaviour, you can be liberated by passionately pursuing Christ as your sole desire. Instead of being consumed by lustful thoughts, or looking for intimacy with men who are not and will not be your husband, how much better is it if you can say, with the Psalmist, that 'My soul thirsts for God, for the living God. When can I go and meet with God?' (Psalm 42:2 NIV)

Men

Protect your sisters

Men: Just as there are ways that women can help you in your battle for sexual purity, there are things that you can do to help your sisters in Christ with theirs.

First, understand that they are wired differently to you, and do not believe the lie that they don't struggle with purity. If you haven't read parts of this chapter, I encourage you to read them to help you gain an understanding of what your Christian sisters are battling.

You may have noticed that women seem able to get emotionally attached in a far quicker and deeper way than you can—especially if you are spending both quantity and quality time with someone. If you have no intention of pursuing a relationship with her, it is important that you don't engage her in frequent and intimate conversation. Remember that this is a woman's weak spot and she is likely to receive messages that you never intended to give.

It's easy to write them off as crazy, but they're not and thinking of them in this way can be very damaging.

Understand the power of your words. You probably already know that women love to talk, but you perhaps are not aware of the power of conversation for a woman. Here are some thoughts from Hayley DiMarco, author of *The Woman of Mystery:*

> I loved his mind and his verbal adoration. For those few hours I felt truly special and accepted, and it was incredible. We connected in ways that only words can connect two people. Yes, I am pretty sure that talking is an aphrodisiac to a woman in love… when it comes to relationships, the more words I share with a person, the more connected I feel to him or her.[2]

She goes on to say that 'talking can be a powerful tool in the hand of a man who wants to win the heart of a woman',[3] but I would add that talking can be a destructive tool in the hand of a man who has no intention of giving his heart to a woman. If you have no intention of pursuing a woman, then you have no right either to her body or to her heart and the depth of her emotions. As Jeremy Clark says, 'Emotional intimacy should be reserved for certain times and relationships. That's why you must protect yourself and others by setting boundaries for your emotional zone'.[4]

Cultivate same-gender deep spiritual friendships

One of the big challenges that I've noticed for men in this area is the ease with which they can open up to women. Many men find it difficult to share the deep things of life, or their personal struggles, with other men, and greatly appreciate the nurturing and non-judgemental conversational environment that women provide.

Men, this sadly often means that without intending to, you are using women for your own emotional gain. Imagine this scenario: A man, needing to talk, and feeling safe and comfortable with a woman, opens up about what he is struggling with. The woman, takes his openness and deep sharing with her as a sign of trust and even interest, and relishes the time they spend together in deep conversation. Even if she had no interest in him in the beginning, the woman can find herself feeling attached and connected, and begins to imagine that he feels the same. Eventually she is sure that he does, and anticipates the time when he will declare his feelings and ask her out. All too often the man's thoughts weren't on this track at all. In fact, he may have spent the whole time thinking about asking someone else out, while merely appreciating this woman as a good mate who was helping him through a tough time.

Can you see the pain that this can cause? This discrepancy between a man and woman's understanding of where a relationship is headed is all too common. Men, if you need counsel, don't take the easy road and go to a woman. Swallow your pride and make the effort to develop deep spiritual friendships with other men. They will understand your struggles in a way that women cannot and you will protect your Christian sisters from misunderstandings and potential heartbreak.

Our culture far too often confirms the sentiment that 'love is a battlefield'. The field is strewn with broken hearts and sexual compromise. God is calling you away from this path. He is calling you to a high standard of purity, both physically and emotionally. He wants you to renounce idols and cheap fantasies and to guard your hearts and minds. He desires for you to protect your brothers and sisters in Christ, treating them with respect and helping them in their weaknesses.

His call is great, but His grace is sufficient and His ways are perfect. Your culture needs you to answer this call because as you do, you are freed from the entanglement of sin to be the light of the world, a city on a hill bringing a message of hope and redemption to a lost and dying world.

CHAPTER 4

Modesty: Being clothed as godly men and women

Sarah Rose

Sitting on a train, travelling between Sydney and Wollongong, I found it fascinating watching the different people come and go from the various stations along the way. Two women, in particular, caught my attention.

The first, probably a university student, was covered from head to toe and was wearing a blue, patterned hijab—a symbol of Arab modesty. The rest of her attire, however, seemed like a contradiction. A long sleeved black top was worn beneath a figure hugging black dress, which would have appeared scandalously short had she not been wearing semi-opaque stockings. On her feet she wore high, black stiletto shoes, with silver spikes studded over the heels. I found myself wondering about her reasons for dressing that way. She seemed to be ticking the modesty boxes by covering up, but her overall appearance suggested the opposite.

The second woman boarded some time later. In stark contrast, she wore short board shorts and a bikini top. While this would be common on east-coast beaches, it seemed blatantly out of place on a train.

I found it fascinating that two women, who were so opposite in their attire, could both appear to be pushing the boundaries. It made me wonder: Is modesty more about the heart than the skin?

The culture

If you're like me, you've probably found modesty to be one of the most difficult issues for young Christians to work through. The Bible isn't black and white about it and therefore everyone seems to have a different view on 'how little is too little'. On top of that, the standards always seem to be changing. I remember when I was a child, knee high boots were associated with hookers. These days, just about every woman I know wears them, and no one bats an eyelid.

As Christians, we agree that modesty is important, but we're completely lost on how to define it, and our varying definitions often result in judgement. Because modesty is visible, it stands slightly apart from other areas of our sexuality. It's very easy to point out other people's faults, while ignoring our own. How many times have you gossiped about someone, or looked down on them for what they were wearing, while at a later time excusing yourself for similar choices? I know I've been guilty!

It is always possible to find someone who dresses less modestly than you do, so it's easy to let yourself off the hook. As you read this chapter are you willing to be open to what God wants to say to you? Are you willing to set aside the standards and choices of others, and focus on how God may desire to change you? If you are, I believe that God can use you greatly, because modesty is not a petty issue. I think it's one that can have a big impact on our culture.

Over the last fifty years, the western world has experienced an explosion in the sexualisation of women. That billboard you drove past yesterday advertising women's lingerie would have been scandalous fifty years ago, but is just normal today. The media and fashion industries know that the sexy image sells and they are using it to their best advantage. This means that fashion is becoming much more of a moral issue than ever before. When a culture allows its morality to slide, there are inevitable consequences.

The so-called 'Women's Liberation' movement has pushed for a woman's right to be, do and wear anything she wants to, but it has given very little thought to the actual consequences connected with the flaunting of female sexuality. Are you grasping the significance of this? The sexualisation of women is not liberating them, but actually enslaving and objectifying them.

Princeton University did a study in which they discovered that when presented with images of bikini clad women, men were more likely to view them as objects to be used, rather than as independent people with thoughts and feelings. [1]

While sexual objectification and modesty have long been considered a woman's issue, we cannot ignore the fact that men too are being increasingly pressured to conform to physical ideals. The gym-junkie culture means that we are seeing almost as many half-naked selfies of men on Facebook as we are of women, and men are becoming more and more preoccupied with sculpting, flaunting, tanning and dressing their bodies to gain the attention and approval of others.

The tragedy is that even Christians are succumbing to the lies that the sexualisation of their bodies is an expression of freedom and is not a big moral issue. Let's face it guys and girls, do you actually *want* to dress modestly? Modesty has long been associated with drabness. People picture long, un-shapely dresses, socks with sandals and a rejection of fashion. Modesty seems to represent words such as 'boring, plain, prudish and conservative,' in a world that is crying out for 'exciting, sexy, attractive and risqué'.

Even if you know that Christians *should* be modest, how many of these objections have you heard or even used yourself?

- How am I supposed to attract the opposite sex if I dress like a prude?
- Men are surrounded by sexualized images all the time. What I wear won't even affect them.
- If they're having impure thoughts, that's not my responsibility.
- It's just fashion.
- It's all relative to culture, and in our culture it's not considered immodest.
- God made my body like this, and I should be proud of it.
- If I don't dress like that my boyfriend will be looking at other women rather than me.
- I'm a man, so it's not immodest of me to flaunt my body.

Most of these objections contain elements of valid concern; modesty is not a black and white issue, but they also have something else in common. They are all concerned with *my* rights and *my* desires. They represent a fundamental misunderstanding of God's intention behind modesty. As you will see, the call to modesty is not intended to limit you, but to be an expression of your freedom; to enable you to live in the beautiful and exciting way that God created you to live.

Pure Love

As Christians we can no longer excuse ourselves from discussions of modesty as though our current social climate has made it a non-issue. As much as ever, God is calling you to be modest in a world that scorns it and cries for the opposite. Because here's the thing: Modesty is more about what's going on on the inside than it is about what you look like on the outside. So, are you willing to ask God what He has to say to you, knowing that He desires freedom, not bondage for you?

The Scripture

At first, what the Bible says about modesty seems unclear and confusing. In fact, we can even find it a bit unsatisfying. As fallen people, we tend to gravitate towards a list of rules or standards that we cannot only work towards ourselves, but use as a measuring stick by which to judge others.

Not surprisingly though, as we dig deeper, we discover that God has a lot to say on this issue, just perhaps not in the way that we would expect.

Physical beauty is a good thing, but it's powerful too

Often, when a woman thinks of being modest, she associates it with being unattractive. In discussions about modesty, physical beauty seems to get a pretty bad rap and it is important for us to understand that God actually loves outer beauty.

Many women are acclaimed for their beauty throughout the Bible. When we read of women like Rebekah, it is almost as though her physical beauty is a virtue, and in some ways it is. The beauty of a woman is a reflection of the beauty of God himself, and he made beauty to be enjoyed.

Throughout the Bible we see many examples of the ways in which beauty was made to captivate a man. Sarah, Rebekah, Rachel and Esther were some of the women whose beauty is specifically mentioned and we see, quite explicitly in Song of Songs, the way in which a woman's body and physical beauty is used in a beautiful dance of seduction with her lover. Verses 10 and 11 of chapter one even make mention of outer adornment: 'your cheeks are lovely with ornaments, your neck with strings of jewels. We will make for you ornaments of gold, studded with silver.'

Modesty does not mean rejecting physical beauty, but it does mean understanding that God's design in it is not just ornamental. Beauty is powerful, and it is this very power that makes the issue of modesty a significant one.

The allure of a woman's body is like fire: beautiful and influential in the right context, but dangerous and destructive when used wrongly.

These women used their outer beauty to attract and captivate their husbands, but the Bible also mentions women whose outer beauty was a factor in men's lust and eventual downfall. In fact Proverbs warns young men against lusting after and being captivated by the beauty of an immoral woman (6:24-25).

Being beautiful is a wonderful thing, but as a woman, you need to understand the power that comes with your beauty. Powers of seduction, while right and good between a husband and wife, become dangerous and destructive when used outside of God's intent.

Now might be a good time for you to reflect on how you use the physical beauty God has given you. Do you sometimes fall into the temptation to use it to incite the lust of a man who is not your husband? It's a very easy trap to fall in to, but one that can be overcome when you decide to focus on a type of beauty that God says is far more important.

There's something more important than outer beauty

The apostle Paul is one of the writers who address the issue of modesty most explicitly in the Bible. In First Timothy 2, he commends women to 'adorn themselves in respectable apparel, with modesty and self-control, not with braided hair and gold or pearls or costly attire, but with what is proper for women who profess godliness—with good works' (v9-10).

It's easy to get hung up on the specifics, to focus on the braided hair, gold and pearls, but this causes us to miss the point. Earlier in the chapter, Paul's focus was on preaching the gospel and reaching the unsaved. He was reminding the women of who they were, and what their mission was. While their culture, much like our own, may have been very focused on appearance, Paul was reminding the women, that if they claim to be godly, their adornment or beauty should be evident more through their character and good works, than through their flashy appearance. While we like to focus on the external, God goes straight to the heart. He knows that it is far too easy for us, like the Pharisees, to '…outwardly appear righteous to others but within [be] full of hypocrisy and lawlessness' (Matthew 23:28a).

Apparently, in the first century church, women were dressing themselves up in such a way as to call attention to themselves, their beauty and their wealth. Their braided hair, studded with pearls and gold was attracting attention to themselves, rather than Christ. In a society in which both the very rich and the very poor were joining the family of God, there was potential for great discrepancy in attire. [2] If the women then were anything like the women today, this could have been a point of comparison and jealousy, taking away from the gospel of Christ. Is this something you can relate to in your own church? How much of your attention or conversation is focused on the outward appearance of others, rather than on gathering to worship and encourage each other in godliness?

Peter also spoke of the beautiful women of the Bible and said, 'For this is how the holy women who hoped in God used to adorn themselves, by submitting to their own husbands, as Sarah obeyed Abraham, calling him lord' (1 Peter 3:5-6). Thousands of years after she had died, Sarah, a woman of great physical beauty, was commended not for her outer adornments, but for her beautiful character that manifested itself in godly submission to her husband.

On several occasions in the Bible beauty and character are compared. Proverbs says that 'Charm is deceitful, and beauty is vain, but a woman who fears the Lord is to be praised' (31:30), and it even compares a beautiful woman with no discretion, to a gold ring in a pig's snout! (11:22)

Outward appearance can be deceptive. Even the angel Lucifer was known to be 'perfect in beauty' (Ezekiel 28:12), and yet this concealed a proud heart that led to great destruction. Women who pursue external beauty above internal beauty are missing the point of where a person's true value lies.

It's important that the men don't escape attention here. While the above verses are directed at women, the sentiment applies to men as well. Men in our society are becoming increasingly focused on appearance, and, like women, they can become tempted to allow the preoccupation with the external to overshadow what is really important in life.

As Christians we must all remember our purpose. Being beautiful or attractive may be a gift, but it must never be our main focus. Our internal beauty and Christ-like character are lasting and will enable us to impact our culture for Christ.

Modest in speech and action

The topic of modesty is often limited to a woman's clothing; however, the book, *Modest: Men and Women Clothed in the Gospel*, claims that modesty is a virtue grounded in respect and is made evident not only in dress, but also in speech and behaviour.[3]

It is not surprising that the Bible also has something to say about women who may be considered immodest in the way they speak and act. Peter talks about the beauty of a gentle and quiet spirit (1 Peter 3:4) and Paul talks of the modest woman being clothed in good deeds (1 Timothy 2:10). Colossians encourages God's chosen people to clothe themselves with compassionate hearts, kindness, humility, meekness and patience (3:12). These things point to individuals who are not brash or flirtatious, who do not laugh at, or make crude jokes and whose actions reflect their inner purpose, dignity and modesty.

The modest woman is the polar opposite of the adulteress mentioned in Proverbs, who is 'dressed like a prostitute and [has] crafty intent. (She is loud and defiant, her feet never stay at home; now in the streets, now in the squares, at every corner she lurks)' (Proverbs 7:10-12 NIV). Can you picture this woman? She draws attention to herself not only by what she wears on the outside, but also by her loud voice and self-seeking, defiant actions. The modest woman is different. Her inner peace and strength enable her to demonstrate gentleness and a quiet spirit. This does not mean that a modest woman cannot be extroverted, but that her humility and sense of dignity do not allow her personality traits to control her and become self-seeking. When you reflect on your interactions with others, can you see that there are times that you are not presenting yourself as modest in your speech and actions? If so, thank God that He has revealed this to you, and ask Him to help you reflect His character more.

The Scriptures have a high view of modesty. It directs attention to God rather than self; it protects from temptation; it creates inner, lasting beauty. External modesty is a beautiful reflection of a heart that is focused on God and His ministry.

The call

So how do you live as a virtuous, godly, modest person in a culture that exalts promiscuity and worships external appearance and body image? You realign your heart and thoughts to love God and others.

Focus on what is really important

The most important thing for you, as a Christian, to pursue is Christlikeness.

If you pursue modesty exclusively, you may become outwardly modest, but other areas of your life will be lacking. But if you pursue Christ, you will find that the other things, like modesty, will gradually become part of your character. Modesty is not the way to Christ-likeness; rather it is one of the outcomes of Christ-likeness.

The pursuit of Christ-likeness also prevents you from focusing on rules. Challies and Glenn warn that 'If we reduce modesty to certain rules of dress, we are completely separating the concept of modesty from the work of Jesus Christ.'[4] Being modest will never save you. It won't even earn you more favour with God. You are saved by grace and grace alone. It is important that, as you pursue modesty, you do it out of love, first for God, and second for those around you. If your pursuit of modesty is self-focused—an attempt to seem more spiritual than those around you—then it is not modesty at all, but pride; you have become like the Pharisees who appear spiritual on the outside, but who are unclean on the inside (Matthew 23:27).

Focusing on Christ and not yourself, however, does not mean that you can simply ignore what is going on around you. Christians who are naïve and uninformed can damage the body of Christ, even if their own consciences are clear. Understanding how your actions affect others will help you to demonstrate Christ's love to them better.

Are you aware?

It has been said that ignorance is bliss, and it may well be, but it's often a very selfish form of bliss. Ignorance to your own weaknesses and the impact your actions have on those around you may prevent you from feeling guilty or uncomfortable, but it is neither edifying nor productive.

Are you aware of how much time and money you are spending on your appearance?

Women, beauty is a wonderful gift, but it is never to become your main focus. If you are spending money on expensive clothes that you don't need, or spending hours adorning yourself in front of the mirror as a method of self-validation or a means by which to attract the attention of others, you are missing out on fulfilling your greater purpose.

Likewise, men, have a think about how much time and money you're spending at the gym. Looking after your body is beneficial, but becoming obsessed with image and appearance is not.

Are you aware of where your true value lies?

Women, in particular, feel great pressure to attract the opposite sex through their appearance. But if this is your focus, you are selling yourself short. Your value is not equal to your physical appearance and any man who pursues you for that alone, is not worth your while. As a Christian it should be your character and godliness that makes you beautiful. Spending time cultivating inner beauty will attract a far higher calibre of man than those who run after the external beauty that is fleeting.

Men: are you aware of the struggle that women go through in an appearance-saturated world?

Eric and Leslie Ludy lament that 'most Christian men do not seem to fully appreciate a woman's desire to guard her heart and protect her purity. It's an unending battle for a woman to hold on to her treasure, and then she begins to wonder if it's even worth it. What if guys *aren't* looking for that kind of purity in a woman?'[5]

Christian men, you really need to be aware of what you are attracted to in a woman. You might say that you appreciate modesty and sexual purity and want those qualities in a wife, but if your actions don't match up, you're making it very difficult for your Christian sisters to really see the value in modesty. I've seen Christian women very hurt and discouraged by Christian men who do not seem to see modesty as a desirable virtue in a woman. This significantly undermines the great cost it is for a woman to work to preserve her body and beauty for the enjoyment of one man.

Men: are you aware of how much you flaunt your body when you are around women?

Men often tend to think they're off the hook in this area, because women don't traditionally struggle with the lust of the eyes in the same way that men do. There are two issues with this philosophy:

- ○ Our society has long encouraged women to perv on a man's well-sculpted body, and there are many men who are more than willing to be the subject of this objectification.
- ○ Modesty is much more about your heart than your audience. It is quite possible to behave immodestly, even if no one is looking.

Women: are you aware of the impact your body can have on men?

Many women don't fully understand the way in which God combined the visual stimulation of men and the beauty of the female body to have such a dynamite effect. Be aware that as a woman, you cannot fully comprehend the Christian man's battle for sexual purity. Just because you don't find it sexually provocative, doesn't mean that a man sees it in the same way.

Now surely you are not responsible for the thoughts of a man? No, you are not. But you are responsible for your own thoughts and intent. If you knowingly present yourself in a way that is likely to lead a man into temptation, for your own sense of power and gratification, are you not also guilty of sin?

It's interesting to note Dannah Gresh's observations in her book *Secret Keeper*. From her experience in the advertising industry, she talks about men's natural inclination to 'complete the image' and concludes that 'it's much more tempting for a guy to see a girl dressed in today's skimpy fashions, than it would be to see her naked'.[6]

Some guys tell me that for them, it's less about skin and more about shape. Even when you're covering up, wearing things that closely reveal the curves of your body can be a real trigger for guys struggling with lust. Remember our two women on the train? Both women were dressed in such a way that drew attention to, and sensualised the shape of their bodies, even though one of them was covered from head to toe.

Women, remember what your body is for. First and foremost for the glory of God and secondly, should God give you a husband, for your mutual enjoyment. Jesus said that any lustful desire towards a woman, by a man who is not her husband, is adultery. Sadly, many women present themselves in such a way that they are actually inviting any man to view them in this way.

It can be very challenging for women to grasp the impact that their immodesty can have, or even what should be considered immodest. It can be helpful, if you have Christian fathers or brothers, to ask them about your attire and be willing to take their advice. There are surveys that have been conducted asking Christian guys what particular areas of temptation or struggle are, such as the one at www.therebelution.com. It may also be worthwhile, particularly for married women, to read books such as *Every Man's Battle* by Stephen Arterburn and Fred Stoeker, which offers great insight into the daily battle that men face.

This awareness should not cause you to obsess further over your appearance, but rather to help you bring glory to God by supporting your Christian brothers in their fight for purity.

Are you aware of culture and social trends?

One of the things that make the issue of modesty so challenging is that it is largely influenced by culture. Culture can determine which parts of the body are seen as sexual, and which parts should be covered up. Social trends can change, so that an item of clothing that was once associated with promiscuity (like those knee high boots) is now considered commonplace. This is perhaps the area in which you as a Christian woman are most in need of wisdom and grace. You need to be gracious towards those who don't meet your standards of cultural or social appropriateness. Making the assumption that they are trying to draw sexual attention to themselves is not helpful, and may often be incorrect.

Also be aware that things that you wear in one context may not be appropriate in another. An Australian woman who insists on exerting her right to dress like an Australian in a much more conservative country or culture, is not being modest.

Are you aware that some accepted social trends or fashions have been created for the purpose of arousing desire in men?

Sometimes the culture can become so immodest and so sexually saturated, that a Christian is called not only to be somewhat more modest than the culture's standards, but drastically so. Fashions and trends may be commonplace with 'everyone doing it' or 'everyone wearing it', but it may be inappropriate for a Christian woman.

Are there items in your wardrobe, which you'd assumed were 'just fashion,' but that you can now see are designed to make you appear sexy to men? I know I have to do regular re-evaluations of my wardrobe, and ask myself what message I'm trying to send with what I wear. Sometimes I'm horrified by things I used to wear, and other times I find myself feeling convicted over a new purchase. Slowly I'm learning to thoughtfully evaluate items in the shop change room, before it reaches my closet!

Women: are you aware of where your weaknesses lie?

Ever since the fall of Adam and Eve, one of women's greatest downfalls has been her desire for power. A woman's body and sexuality are very powerful, and women can be greatly tempted to use them. The media has known of and utilized this power in advertising for decades. Gresh claims that the image of a woman's body holds both male *and* female attention longer than any other image.[7] Having this kind of power over people can be a real point of temptation for a woman, but it is a temptation that needs to be surrendered to God. Is this something that you need to reconsider? Are you using the power of your physical allure to manipulate people or draw attention to yourself, rather than using your modesty and godly character to point them to Jesus?

The Bible is clear that God does not look at the outward appearance, but rather at the heart, and as Christians we should follow suit. There is something, however, that is worth remembering for a woman. Your outward dress and appearance is one of the only visual reflections you have of your inward character. An immodestly dressed woman is suggestive of an immodest character, whether that is actually the case or not.

Are you willing to lay down your rights?

In our self-focused culture it's easy to believe that you have the right to do whatever you want with your body, but the Christ-like woman does things differently. She lays down her rights for the sake of others. She realizes that her 'body is the temple of the Holy Spirit' (1 Corinthians 6:19), that she is not her own, that she has been bought with a price. She lays down her rights, so as to glorify God in her body (1 Corinthians 6:20).

Sometimes I find this kind of surrender difficult. For me it means not even trying on that dress that I can see is too short or low cut, even though I know it could look good on me; It means not wearing a bikini to the beach even when everyone else is; It means learning not to judge other women when they wear things that I find to be inappropriate or provocative; Sometimes it has even meant dressing down for church because I knew that my mind was far too consumed with my appearance. There are definite challenges associated with choosing to dress modestly, but there are opportunities too. You have the opportunity to develop your own unique style that is trendy, fashionable and feminine, while still honouring God with your body. Instead of focusing on what you can't or shouldn't wear, look for things that will help you express the unique woman that God has made you to be.

As you surrender to God, you will find that He fills you with a peace and joy that make you wonder why on earth you held so tightly to things that didn't please Him.

Are you willing to lay down your rights in surrender to Him, knowing that He desires your greatest joy?

Are you willing to lay down your rights so that the church can be a place in which a man, weary from his constant battle with purity in a sexually saturated world, can find some refuge, confident that the women around him will dress to prevent extra temptation?

Are you willing to surrender your right to wear some of the new and skimpy fashions?

Are you willing to surrender your right to say and do whatever you please, knowing that there are things that will detract from the glory of God?

As you do these things, you will be cultivating a modest beauty that is far deeper than your external appearance. Modesty is an outward reflection of an inward godly character. Modesty is not about covering up what is beautiful, but rather unveiling what is most beautiful.

CHAPTER 5

Pornography: Killing the monster of lust

Timon Bengtson

Brad grew up in a Christian family. His parents had been very careful to provide the best possible environment for their son growing up. He never had access to any type of pornographic material—either in magazines, movies, on TV or on the internet (they had only one computer in the family room).

But things changed in grade five when he stole his first glimpse on a school camp. One of his friends had brought a Playboy *magazine from home and at night all the boys huddled around, indulging in its forbidden pleasure. He found himself filled with feelings that he had never experienced before—enormous excitement, but also guilt. He knew that he was doing something wrong.*

While that first experience only lasted a few minutes, a door was opened that should have remained closed. Over the next nine years the giant of lust lay dormant —biding its time.

On occasion it stirred and raised its ugly head when Brad would fantasize about what the girls in his class looked like under their clothes, or when he saw a movie or a TV show with a sexually provocative scene, or when he thought back to the day he saw the Playboy. *However, for most of his childhood and adolescent years it was far from the forefront of his mind. But, little did he realize, that the sleeping giant of lust was about to awaken and he would be in for the fight of his life.*

When Brad left to go to university he moved out of home and into a dorm room. For the first time in his life he had the freedom to surf the Internet in whatever waters he wished. Where would he go? Immediately, those feelings that he had when he was ten, mixed with a curiosity about what he was missing out on, flooded his mind. And, with one click, he headed down a pathway that would lead to addiction.

For the next couple of hours he was glued to the screen. When he finished he was filled with shame and a sense of guilt that he had never experienced. He scolded himself for what he had done. He thought about what his parents, or even other people in his church would think if they saw him. He made a promise to God and to himself that he would never indulge in this secret sin again. He made a promise that this would be the final time. However, one week later when he was all by himself and bored, he did it again. Once again, he felt shame and guilt. Once again he scolded himself—and promised that this time he would make especially sure that he would never do it again. It only took two days for his resolve to break.

Fast-forward two years and Brad is stuck in a malicious cycle. He wakes up each morning ashamed of what he has done and looked at the night before. He makes all sorts of promises to God that he is going to change, that he is never going to look at pornography again. With all the strength that he can muster he tries to self-atone for what he has seen and done. He tries to silence his guilty conscience by resolving to make it up to God. He vows that he will try harder, read his Bible more and be more devoted to God than he has ever been. However, with each repeated failure he is starting to become more and more numb, and more and more afraid that he will never change. He has no ministry effectiveness, draws away from fellowship with others and does not feel like his prayers are answered at all. The giant of lust, fuelled by pornography, is winning the war.

The culture

Brad's story is not an uncommon one. Researcher Simon Lajeunesse claims that nowadays the 'majority of males have viewed pornography by the time they were ten.' He found that '90% of pornography is consumed on the Internet, while 10% comes from video stores. On average, single men watch pornography three times a week for 40 minutes. Those who are in committed relationships watch it on average 1.7 times a week for 20 minutes.'[1] Viewing pornography is quickly becoming the preferred pastime of most men. And it is not only men, but also women who are being affected by the pornographic world in which we live. For those who may be sceptical, recent statistics tell us that 53% of UK women read erotica novels at least occasionally[2], 51% of female students surveyed in Oxford (UK) said they viewed porn[3], 40% of women under the age of 35 have sent sexually explicit selfies to themselves or others[4], and one in three visits to porn sites are women.[5] In fact according to ZeeNews, India, 30% of data transferred on the Internet is porn.[6] These statistics are distressingly high, and the stats for men are much higher. What should sadden us even more, is that the issue is equally rife amongst Christians.

Like Brad, many Christians find themselves trapped in a cycle that renders them ineffective in ministry, plagued with guilt and unable to form deep and trusting relationships with members of the opposite sex in the way that God intended.

The good news is that lust is not a new beast. It has waged war with humanity for centuries and for centuries men and women have turned to the Scriptures to find the hope, strength and power to win the fight.

The Scripture

Defining pornography

There are many materials out there that may be morally neutral in and of themselves, but they can still incite lust in a man or woman, becoming a vehicle by which they commit adultery in their hearts. Something that might be completely acceptable for one person might become a source of temptation and lust for another. Pornography, however, is more than just an inactive vehicle. It is not morally neutral. In the case of pornography, its very existence is wrong.

Many people like to see pornography as an art form. They justify its existence in the name of art. However, I propose there is a fundamental factor present in the creation of pornography that separates the porn industry from much of the rest of the art world. That factor, which makes all the difference, is intent.

Pornography has a very specific intent: to use explicit imagery in order to provoke lust in the viewer. The world of porn is not willing to take a back seat and settle for being distantly appreciated. No, this multi-billion dollar industry relies on its ability to capture the viewer, drawing them deeper and deeper into its web, creating an ever-growing need for more. The porn industry is driven by lust, therefore it seeks primarily to incite lust.

While other art forms may arouse lust in some people, if they were not created with that intent, they probably are not intrinsically sinful. Pornography, however, is intrinsically sinful. Not only does it have intent that is contrary to the teaching of the Bible, but its composition also flies in the face of all that God says is good. Pornography celebrates adultery and glorifies prostitution and sexual violence.

Porn's impact, however, goes far beyond intent. Are you willing to open your heart to what the Bible has to say about pornography? Even if you can't see its destructive influence on your life right now, the Bible gives clear reasons why engaging with this kind of material is wrong and why Christians should abstain from it.

Pornography is a distortion of human sexuality

God created sex. Genesis tells us that God created male and female, including all their organs, and said that it was very good (Genesis 1:31). We find sex pleasurable and fun because God created it that way. Genesis also tells us that through their sexual union, the married couple becomes 'one flesh' (Genesis 2:24). He created sexual intimacy as a covenant act that demonstrates the commitment of one partner to the other. A further building of intimacy comes when the husband and wife give each other, exclusively, the gift of their nakedness.

Pornography, both by its nature and intent, is a distortion of these things. It sells sex as something that can be consumed without covenant. It celebrates adultery and fornication. The nakedness in pornography invades the exclusivity of nakedness within a marriage. Therefore, instead of building up the covenant of marriage, pornography tears it down.

As Challies says 'It tears love from sex, leaving sex as the immediate gratification of base desires. It lives beyond rules and ethics and morality.'[7]

Not only that, but pornography also sets up unrealistic expectations that no man or woman can live up to. Challies again states:

> To give yourself over to pornography is to have your whole perception of sexuality altered, shaped by professional pornographers. You—the man whom God has called to love your wife as Christ loves the church—can be looking at her through the eyes of a pornographer! Would you want Hugh Hefner or some Internet porn-video producer staring at your wife's body, looking it up and down, evaluating her by a set of standards that are literally damnable? And yet there you are looking at her through eyes that men like these have given you. You have handed them your sight. You have handed them a piece of your soul. And they have returned your soul to you battered and filthy, and your sight fractured and distorted.[8]

Not only are the images and scenarios presented in pornographic material *different* from your spouse, but they often stretch the boundaries of any form of true reality. It presents men and women as objects of desire, rather than as whole people who have thoughts, needs, flaws and desires.

Allowing your mind to be filled with distorted ideas of womanhood, manhood and sex can only detract from the beauty of the covenant relationship that God has designed.

Pornography is never static, nor satisfying

Part of pornography's design, as a profitable industry, is to create a desire for more. Pornography gives the illusion of satisfaction, but in reality it carves out a deeper hole in your heart, demanding more in your next attempt to fill it. Galatians 6:7-8 warns that 'whatever one sows, that will he also reap. For the one who sows to his own flesh will from the flesh reap corruption'. Not only does an appetite for pornography fail to fill a person, but it also sows seeds that will grow into a harvest of corruption. In the same way that you cannot serve both God and money (Matthew 6:24), a heart that loves pornography is a heart that is turned from loving and serving God. A heart turned from loving and serving God is left open to be consumed by many other forms of destructive pleasure.

Pornography has a more sinister side

Pornography also has another, arguably more sinister, side that further confirms its sinfulness. Much of the world's pornography has been created using men, women and even children, who have been forced into sexual slavery and who lead lives of oppression, addiction, and violence. As Christians we should be fighting for the freedom of these people, not indulging in their exploitation.

Pornography attacks your ability to love your family

I heard a story about a young girl in a Sunday school class who responded when the teacher asked the class for prayer requests. She told the teacher that they needed to pray for the women in the pictures in her daddy's closet. The teacher asked her why. She responded that they needed to ask God to give them clothes because they had none on.

Whether you are married or not, this story illustrates how pornography can have a devastating effect on families and marriages. Do not think that just because you may be unmarried now, that this is not relevant to you. The habits you form now, will likely be the habits you take into a future marriage.

It is not just the possibility that your family could be exposed to pornography in your home that makes it detrimental, but how it affects and changes you and the way you will relate to your family.

Pornography has the unique power to damage your marriage and your family because it will draw you away from others and into a tiny world of self-gratification. It is a kind of sexual expression that makes your appetites much larger even as your world gets smaller.[9] While you should be thinking about the needs of your family and the ways you can love them, instead, you will become consumed with satisfying your own lusts. The time, energy and resources that should be spent on loving your husband or wife and caring for the needs of your children will be spent on yourself. This can lead to men and women who, instead of pursuing their marital partners, have retreated into their tiny worlds of lust and the intimacy in the marriage has evaporated. Further, how many fathers have forfeited the blessings of fatherhood because, instead of leading their families, they have been consumed with seeking their own pleasure?

Pornography will rob you of spiritual vitality

Pornography will ruin your intimacy with the Almighty. In the Sermon on the Mount Jesus said 'blessed are the pure in heart for they shall see God' (Matthew 5:8). Sexually purity brings with it the blessing of closeness with your heavenly Father. Knowing that you are living in the centre of His will for your life and experiencing His divine pleasure and presence in your life is the greatest reward. David, in Psalm 84:10, said that it is better to spend one day in his house, than one thousand elsewhere. Pornography will rob you of this privilege. You will become wrapped in a world of shame and guilt. You will be focused only on yourself and imprisoned in sin. All of your prayers will become prayers of confession, rather than prayers of praise and adoration. You will not be able to enjoy corporate worship and fellowship with other Christians, because in your heart you know that you are living as a hypocrite.

I remember the first time that I confessed to a group of other believers that I had been viewing pornography. It was freeing. God desires truth in the inmost parts (Psalm 51:6) and when you start confessing the truth of what you have done and start living according to God's Word, you will be on the path to freedom. For me, the day that I confessed to a group of other men was the day that I started down the path to freedom in this area of my life.

The call

Lust is not new; men and woman have been battling it since the fall of humanity. As Paul planted churches among the Hellenistic world in the first century, one of the major issues was sexual purity. In 1 Thessalonians 4:2-8, he outlines two principles that will help us in our battle against lust and pornography.

Principle 1: Embrace God's standard of sexual purity

The first principle Paul gives us in this passage is our need to embrace God's standard of sexual purity. Paul says, 'for this is the will of God, your sanctification, that you abstain from sexual immorality.' We need to stop making excuses for looking at lust-provoking material. It is God's will that we be sexually pure. It is so easy to justify looking at soft porn, saying things like 'that's what guys do' or 'I want to know how to please my husband', but we must actually embrace God's standard.

Part of embracing God's standard of purity demands developing a hatred for pornography. It is vile and destructive, immoral and dishonest, but it is one thing to *know* that it is loathsome and quite another to actually loathe it. The Bible instructs us to 'abhor what is evil; hold fast to what is good' (Romans 12:9). The word 'abhor' is a strong one. It means to 'regard with extreme repugnance or aversion; to detest utterly'.[10] There is barely a harsher word that could be used to describe the absolute hatred we are to have for that which is evil. As we begin to see sin as God sees it, our hearts should be changed to have a deep revulsion and loathing towards it. Instead of seeing pornography as forbidden pleasure, the Christian is to see it for what it is: disgusting and destructive sin. Learning to hate pornography is a vital step in learning to overcome the desire for it. As Tim Challies says:

> You will never stop until you begin to see the monstrous nature of the sin you are committing. You will never stop until the sin is more horrifying to you than the commission of sin is enjoyable. You will need to hate that sin before you can find freedom from it. That means you need more grace. You need to cry out to be changed so you do see the monstrous nature

of this sin, and then you need to act, in faith that God will meet you with grace as you seek to cut off the pornography and begin the reset.[11]

The second part of the passage calls us not only to hate what is evil, but to 'hold fast to what is good'. Redefining your understanding of sex helps in the battle against lust.

While the porn industry portrays sex as a consumer good that is selfish in its focus, the Bible presents a different and liberating view. Sex is good. God, as the creator and designer of sex, is the one most qualified to instruct us on the best possible environment for sex to thrive. From the beginning, God has ordained the exclusive covenant of marriage as the most glorious, exciting and fulfilling way to enjoy sex. Once we begin to know and trust God as the giver, we can better understand the gift. The world presents us with the lie that God is holding out on us; that they have found better and more thrilling ways for sex to be enjoyed. But the world did not create sex, nor do they know the intricacies of the human heart. God, who in the beginning created sex to be 'very good', knows what He's talking about. Trusting in God's wisdom and seeing sex as a means by which we can bring Him glory, changes our tastes and desires.

Embracing God's standard of purity for our lives will involve repentance. If you have been viewing pornography regularly do not be deceived, God is not mocked, what you will sow you will also reap (Galatians 6:7-8). Right now you need to stop. Right now you need to ask God to help you see the horrendous nature of pornography. You need to hate what is evil. Right now you need to ask the Holy Spirit to help you to grieve over what you have been involved with. Ask him to renew your mind and give you God's perspective on sexuality. Ask him to give you a love for

God that will drive out your love for this sin. At the end of our book is an extended section on how the gospel can change you and how to practise true repentance. Maybe, right now you need to turn to the end of our book and read that section.

Principle 2: Learn how to control your sexual appetites

Paul says, 'you should abstain from sexual immorality, that each one of you should know how to control his own body in holiness and honour' (1 Thessalonians 4:3-4). Remember, Paul was writing to people who were swimming in a sea of sexual immorality. While self-control is a fruit of the Holy Spirit, it is something that God expects us, empowered by Spirit, to cultivate. So, here are eight Biblical strategies that you can employ to help you learn how to control your sexual appetites:

Strategy 1: Practice true repentance

The pathway to self-control begins with repentance. Repentance involves seeing sin as God sees it, grieving over it, and turning back to God for forgiveness and the grace to change. As you learn how to control your body in a way that is holy and honourable, you will find the need to practice true repentance. You will find that you will not only need to repent once, but more than likely, you will find yourself often coming back to God. But don't get discouraged, you will find that God's grace is more powerful than your sin.

Strategy 2: Confess your sin to others

Confession of sin before others makes it more real. We can easily deceive ourselves when we are battling with our sin in private. However, when we bring our sin out into the light and confess it before others, it gives them the opportunity to minister the gospel into our lives. If you have never confessed the sin of pornography to another person, then I doubt whether you will be able to grow past it. One of my lecturers at Dallas Theological Seminary once said that he had never known anyone who was able to overcome the sin of pornography alone.

Strategy 3: Find an accountability partner

We, as the church, are the body of Christ. If one part of the body is unable to function, the whole body suffers. Therefore, the body must band together to help, nurture and encourage those who are languishing under the weight of pornography. If you are struggling in a silent battle against pornography, look to godly mentors to help you in your battle. The trap of pornography has long been considered so shameful that few have the courage to declare their struggle. If the statistics are correct, however, it is a struggle the majority of people have faced. Be willing to enlist the help of godly men and women. These people are likely no strangers to the fight, and will be able to pray for you, encourage you and keep you accountable. The world tells us that sin must remain hidden; the gospel tells us that all can be brought to light, because Jesus has dealt with the darkness. Have the courage to share your battle with someone and ask to be kept accountable.

Strategy 4: Make no provision or room for it

Paul, in Romans 13:14, states that Christians are to 'put on the Lord Jesus Christ, and make no provision for the flesh to gratify its desires'. All too often we sin because we do not have a practical plan for how we are going to fight against it. At Dallas Theological Seminary we were taught to develop a Planned Biblical Response (PBR). This is a plan for how we make sure that there is no provision for temptation and, when we do encounter temptation, how we are going to respond. A PBR means taking some radical measures to ensure that we are not intentionally putting ourselves into a position to be tempted. I know this is going to be a controversial statement, but I believe that no Christian should own a computer, tablet or smart phone that doesn't have some sort of software that blocks their access to pornography. Furthermore, Christians should think about what TV programs they watch and what movies they see. They might not get aroused in the moment, but images can be stored in your memory and be used by Satan later as a means of attack.

This PBR can also include ways that a person can respond when a good-looking woman (or man) walks down the street and when sexual thoughts arise. In the book, *Every Man's Battle*, the authors suggest that Christian men need to protect two gates where temptation can assault them—the eye gate and the mind gate. They suggest that men make a covenant with their eyes that whenever they see a good looking woman (whether virtually or in real life) they learn to bounce their eyes, not indulging in a second glance. Further, they suggest that when a sexual thought enters their minds, they need to immediately turn it over to God, rather than indulge it.[12]

Strategy 5: Enlist your spouse to help

For married people, the fifth strategy is to enlist your spouse to help you in your fight with pornography. If you have not yet shared your struggle with pornography with your spouse, then I suggest you go to your Pastor and ask for his assistance in doing so. Your sexual sin is a part of your spouse's life. Because God has joined you together as one flesh and you have been sinning against her or him by being unfaithful in your heart, your spouse needs to know and you need to seek his or her forgiveness.

This will do two very important things. First, it will make your sexual sin very real. While it is hidden, you can believe the lie that you are not hurting anyone. But you are. You are hurting yourself and your spouse. I will never forget one of my friends telling me what it was like the first time he told his spouse that he had a problem with pornography. She was absolutely crushed. As most women are very self-conscious about their bodies, it made her feel like she was not loved and that she was not enough for him. He determined that he did not want to keep hurting her in this way.

Further, telling your spouse can enlist his or her help in your fight against pornography. In 1 Corinthians 7:2, Paul states, 'But because of the temptation to sexual immorality, each man should have his own wife and each woman her own husband'. One of the ways to fight against sexual sin is to develop a normal, healthy and consistent sexual relationship in marriage. A limited sex-life within marriage is never an excuse to turn to pornography, but a spouse can really help in the fight against sexual sin by not depriving their husband or wife of sexual intimacy (1 Corinthians 7:5).

Strategy 6: Fill your mind with God's Word

In seminary, one of my professors, the late Howard Hendricks, once said that whenever he was discipling a young man who was struggling with pornography, he would get them into a strict Bible memorization program. He said that your mind can only be focused on one thing at a time and it is best that it be filled with God's Word.

Strategy 7: Replace immorality, with thankfulness

The seventh strategy may not seem to belong, but it is very important. We need to replace immorality with thankfulness. In Paul's radical call to purity in Ephesians 5:3-4 he says:

> … Sexual immorality and all impurity or covetousness must not even be named among you, as is proper among saints. Let there be no filthiness nor foolish talk nor crude joking, which are out of place, *but instead let there be thanksgiving.*

Did you notice what Paul says at the end? We need to replace immorality in our lives with thankfulness. Now why is this? Well, what is at the heart of immorality? What is at the heart of desire to look at pornography? It is a discontentment with what God has given us. So, in order to deal with pornography at its root, we need to replace that discontentment with thankfulness. Heath Lambert writes:

> The only time people are immoral and impure is when they are greedy for things that are immoral and impure. Take away the greedy heart that desires immorality, and those evil actions will also go away. Paul sees something unique about gratitude

91

that has the power to destroy the greedy lust gripping the heart.[13]

So men, maybe one of the strategies that you need to put in place is to thank God for the abundant blessings He has given you. It may be your wife, friends and family or a job or ministry that He is blessing. All of these things are gifts from God, put into your life for your pleasure and edification. Instead of focusing on what your sinful nature craves, cultivate a spirit of thankfulness that focuses on the great things that God has already given you.

Strategy 8: Cultivate an intimate relationship with Jesus

This final strategy is probably the most important. You will never overcome any sin in your life, unless you love Jesus more than your sin. As Paul says in 2 Corinthians 3:18, 'And we all, with unveiled face, beholding the glory of the Lord, are being transformed into the same image from one degree of glory to another'. As we spend time with Jesus and behold his glory, the by-product will be transformation—we will be transformed from one degree of glory to another. The whole reason that we should put off pornography and put on sexual purity is not just because it will bring happiness into our lives. Nor is it just because it will stop hurting our families or spouses. The main reason we should turn away from pornography is because embracing sexual purity makes us more like Jesus and brings glory to our great God. We should turn away from pornography because we love Jesus and want to keep His commands (John 14:21).

CHAPTER 6

Masturbation: Glorifying God with your body

Timon Bengtson

Lachlan is like many young, Christian men. He goes to church each Sunday, is involved in a small group and serves in a ministry. He hopes to get married, but is not desperate. He is serving God and waiting to meet someone with whom he can share the rest of his life. Like most red-blooded young males, Lachlan struggles to maintain purity in the culture in which he lives. But Lachlan's battle with lust is not the same as the other blokes in his church or small group. He doesn't regularly look at pornography on the Internet and he has never even read a Playboy *magazine. But Lachlan does feel the fires of lust. Every now and again (maybe once a month) the sexual tension builds in him to the point where he feels like exploding and so he goes into the bathroom and relieves the pressure. When he first did it, he felt very guilty and remorseful. But he read somewhere on the Internet that as long as it doesn't become habitual it is okay. Lots of people were saying that it had nothing to do with sexual morality; that it was just very clinical.*

Even though Lachlan has used various forms of reasoning to try to quiet his conscience after he does it, he still finds that he cannot sleep, cannot pray and tries to avoid seeing people the next day. If masturbation is so natural, then why does it produce such shame and guilt?

The culture

I (Timon) can really relate to Lachlan's struggle. Growing up in the church there was one word that was rarely ever mentioned. It was the word 'masturbation'. It was a topic that was rarely preached on or even spoken about in church. However, it is an issue that most men and women deal with.

From 'sinful and harmful' to 'natural and good' in 100 years

If you look at the history of western society, you will see an alarming trend. You will notice that attitudes towards masturbation have changed dramatically in 100 years. You have to wonder where the schoolyard myths concerning masturbation originated. In the schoolyard, it was something that you would never admit to doing. And there were all types of myths going around such as: if you masturbated too much you could go blind, or grow hair on your palms or it would stunt your growth. Now of course these myths have no ground in reality, but they do tell us something about people's perceptions of masturbation. In general, they tell us that people viewed masturbation as harmful and wrong, and that they thought practising masturbation could have harmful effects in your life. This was partly because western society had been deeply influenced by the protestant reformation and adopted the morals and values of the Bible concerning sex.

A natural part of adolescent life

Fast-forwarding to today, however, we see that attitudes and values have dramatically changed. In most sexual education courses conducted in public schools, masturbation is taught to be a natural part of adolescence. It is believed that as the human body changes through puberty, we feel the urge to masturbate and this is a natural and healthy part of growing up.

The assumption has been that masturbation is a part of the curiosity and experimentation that comes with adolescence, and in time, most people would grow out of 'unhealthy' patterns of masturbation. In other words, the message being taught is that the guilt and the shame associated with masturbation came from the Victorian Era's negative suppression of sexuality and that we should now embrace the practice as healthy and normal. Further, some teach that masturbation can be useful in relationships. If one partner wants more sex than another, it is suggested that masturbation can fulfil that need, thus leading to a more harmonious relationship.[1]

Even many prominent Christian authors and teachers have adopted this perspective on masturbation. James Dobson, a popular Christian author and teacher, stated:

> It is my opinion that masturbation is not much of an issue with God. It is a normal part of adolescence that involves no one else. It does not cause disease. It does not produce babies, and Jesus did not mention it in the Bible. I'm not telling you to masturbate, and I hope you won't feel the need for it. But if you do, it is my opinion that you should not struggle with guilt over it. Why do I tell you this? Because I deal with so many Christian young people who are torn apart with guilt over masturbation; they want to stop and just can't. I would like to help you avoid that agony.[2]

Dr Dobson is not alone in his opinion. When I was back in seminary, a pastor at the church I was attending told a group of guys that he thought that masturbation was not a sin. He said that it could be a sin if you looked at pornography, but if you just went into a toilet and relieved yourself quietly, it wasn't a sin.

Further, when I was younger I went to a church that had a young adult ministry. One night, some of the guys got to talking about sexuality and masturbation in particular. One of the guys, who was very outspoken, said very openly that he masturbated and did not see anything wrong with it. He told the whole group that it was okay to masturbate and think about girls naked, as long as you did not put faces to their bodies. He said that as long as you were only thinking about faceless bodies, then it was not lust and therefore not a sin. I have serious reservations about his stance.

We can see that in 100 years, masturbation has gone from being considered sinful and harmful, to being seen as healthy and good. But when did this change begin to occur? What was it that began to sway people towards thinking that masturbation was good and healthy?

One of the most influential forces in the sexual revolution of last century was a man by the name of Alfred Kinsey. He was the first ever sexologist. According to author Albert Mohler, he was one of the most controversial figures in American history and wrote a pioneering book called *Sexual Behaviour in the Human Male*. Molher notes that:

> Indiana University was to establish the Kinsey Institute for Research in Sex, Gender, and Reproduction, and the name 'Kinsey' would be associated with progressivism in sex education, opposition to traditional sexual morality, and liberation from fixed concepts of 'normal' when dealing with human sexuality.[3]

Kinsey posited that masturbation was an instinctive behaviour, citing the results from the Gallup Poll surveys that showed how common the practice was in the United States. Because a majority of people said that they masturbated with some regularity, Kinsey said that it must be a normal part of human sexuality.

It doesn't take much, however, to see how faulty this line of reasoning is. Lying and stealing are also common practices of humanity. Do we then propose that these activities are normal and, therefore, acceptable practices for humanity? Acceptable practices, or morality, especially for Christians, should never be based on public opinion or majority rule, but rather on God's Word.

The Scripture

Is masturbation sexual?

This may seem like a strange question to ask, but it is an important one. Much of the confusion about masturbation comes because you do not find the word 'masturbation' in the Bible. This has led many to believe that masturbation is a morally neutral practise, meaning that in and of itself it is not wrong. Though masturbation is not directly addressed, it is not right to assume that God has nothing to say on the topic. In fact, if masturbation is a sexual activity, we find that the Bible speaks openly and extensively about it.

Some of those who argue that masturbation is a morally neutral practise claim that it is possible to masturbate without sexual thoughts, in particular thoughts relating to another person. Irrespective of whether this is true, I would argue

97

that masturbation in and of itself is a sexual act. It involves the sexual organs, with the purpose of creating or simulating a sexual experience, climaxing in orgasm. There is little doubt that masturbation is a sexual act. The question, then, is what the Bible has to say about sexual acts, and whether there is a distinction made between those involving others and those that don't.

Is it wrong to masturbate?

God created sexuality to be a beautiful expression of self-giving love within marriage. It was to be a shared experience that bound a husband and wife in a one-flesh union. The idea that sexual expression or experience could be legitimate without the involvement of another person clearly falls outside of God's design. The 'marriage bed' is something that is repeatedly honoured and protected throughout the Scriptures and sexual activity outside of the marriage covenant is frequently addressed.

The Bible contains many passages that deal with sexuality and sexual practise and these should inform your conscience, as to whether it is right to engage in masturbation.

Paul, in Colossians 3:5, states that Christians should put to death 'sexual immorality, impurity, passion, evil desire and covetousness, which is idolatry'. The first three concepts in this verse are particularly important regarding masturbation and we'll look at each in turn.

1) Sexual immorality

In older translations of the Bible 'sexual immorality' was simply translated 'fornication', however most Bible scholars agree that the term actually denotes any 'kind of illegitimate sexual practice',[4] that is, any sexual practice outside of God's standard. It is hard to imagine masturbation not being included in this category. As we have already discussed elsewhere in this book, sexual love is satisfying when it is focused outward, when each marriage partner is finding their joy in meeting the needs of the other. Masturbation, on the other hand, is not focused outward, but inward. It is inherently selfish. The focus of many when they masturbate is upon self and the fulfilment of their needs. Jeffrey Black writes:

> The goal of pornography and masturbation is to create a substitute for intimacy. Masturbation is sex with yourself. If I'm having sex with myself, I don't have to invest myself in another person. People who are 'addicted' to pornography aren't so much addicted to lurid material as they're addicted to self-centeredness. They're committed to serving themselves, to doing whatever they can to find a convenient way not to die to self, which is the nature of companionship in a relationship.[5]

Black's comments are compelling. If masturbation becomes a substitute for God's design in sex, then it must be considered sexual immorality.

2) Impurity

The term 'impurity' denotes a 'man (or woman) whose actions are determined by his commitment to his natural lusts'.[6] I believe that when most people engage in masturbation their actions are being determined by their natural and sinful lusts. For most, masturbation is not just a physical act, but is a result of a sinful desire that has been aroused or stimulated. For example, masturbation is typically associated with pornography or mental fantasy. Author Joshua Harris agrees and writes:

> I know there are Christians who claim they can masturbate without lusting. They say they think nonsexual thoughts and do it merely for release. It's not my place to judge the hearts of these people. I can only speak from my own experience when I say that I highly doubt this is possible. What I've seen is that lust was always present in a significant way either leading up to or during the act... Maybe I can convince myself I'm not lusting in that moment, but the likelihood is that my heart is deceiving me.[7]

As you search your own hearts, can you honestly say that you have always been free of any form of lust while you masturbated? If what Harris says is true, then masturbation is one of the things that God warns us against in Colossians.

3) Passion

In the context of this passage, the word 'passion' denotes 'shameful passion which leads to sexual excesses'.[8] Why do you think there is shame often associated with masturbation? I would like to suggest that it is because our consciences know that we are being selfish when we are masturbating and that it is the fruit of a shameful passion that is being aroused.

Therefore, although the Scriptures do not specifically mention masturbation, it is reasonable to consider that it will fall under the umbrella of these terms—as an immoral practice, as an act of impurity or as motivated by a shameful passion.

Does masturbation keep you from greater sin?

Many Christians I know practice habitual masturbation because they reason that it keeps them from greater sexual sin. For example, some Christians reason that 'if I allow myself to masturbate then I won't look at porn, or end up going too far with my girlfriend or boyfriend.' However, I believe that this dangerous because it is a misunderstanding of what sin is and the way that it works.

Sin does not just involve outward actions, but comes from the inward intentions of the heart. Jesus says in Mark 7:21, that our outward actions proceed from our hearts. He says 'For from within, out of the heart of man, come evil thoughts, sexual immorality etc.' He is saying that we sin outwardly because of the inward desires of our heart; because in that moment we are loving someone or something more than God. Most of the time, I have found that when it comes to sexual immorality, we sin because we are placing our pleasure above God. We violate God's standards of sexual morality because we want our own sexual desires to be fulfilled more than we want to honour God.

So to think that masturbation will keep you from greater sexual sin is a fallacy. You cannot practise one sin in the hope that it will keep you from another. In order to stop sexual immorality in your life you must deal with your heart. You must come back to God and repent of putting the idol of pleasure above Him and love Jesus more than you love sin.

Is masturbation harmful?

As we have seen in the opening of this chapter, many people would disagree with me and say that masturbation is not harmful and therefore should be embraced as normal. You must remember however, that not everything that is harmful has immediate or obvious consequences. You must always trust the Word of God above your own experiences. Further, I have found that for the majority of people I have counselled in my pastoral ministry, and for me personally, habitual masturbation has been very destructive.

Firstly, masturbation is rarely static and typically leads to further sexual enslavement. Jesus' half-brother James tells us that we sin because we are tempted and lured away by our lusts. If we give in to temptation it will give birth to sin, and sin when it is fully grown brings forth death (James 1:14-15). I have found in my own life, and in the lives of the men I have journeyed with, that when we masturbate it does not just stop there. Because I am married I might say that I masturbate to thoughts about my wife (and how can having sexual thoughts about your husband or wife be wrong?) but unfortunately it rarely stops there—sin is never satisfied.

This is equally true for young men and women who are single. Many Christians encounter their own sexuality and discover masturbation at a young age, and it is tragic that they often feel they have nowhere to turn for wise counsel. This means that many young Christians are engaging in a practise that can open the floodgates of their sexuality. Instead of guarding their hearts and waiting until it's time, young people who masturbate open the doors to sexual temptation long before they are in a position to join with someone in a marital union. If you feed lust and engage in sexual actions before marriage it invites in sin and sin will bring forth death. John Owen, a seventeenth century puritan, used to say that 'we must be killing sin or it will be killing us'.[9] We are never static in our fight with our sin—sin will either be defeating us, or we will be putting it to death by the Spirit (Romans 8:13).

Secondly, I have found that masturbation is harmful because it is inherently selfish and leads people into isolation. Rather than pursuing intimacy with their spouse it can draw people to live in their own private little worlds. Harris writes:

> Sometimes 'solo sex' seems easier, even more pleasurable, than the work involved with maintaining intimacy with your spouse and unselfishly seeking to give him or her pleasure. But a husband or wife who turns to masturbation in marriage becomes a rival to his or her own spouse. The act of masturbation draws them away from each other.[10]

We do not know how many relationships have started down the path of destruction due to masturbation.

Finally, and most importantly, if masturbation is sinful then it will lead to a loss of intimacy with God. Probably the greatest tragedy of the western church is that instead of people enjoying lives of closeness with God, many live in shame and guilt rather than in the fullness of what God wants for them. God does not require things of us in His moral law that bring us harm. One of the greatest mysteries of God's character is the way in which He works both for his glory and our benefit. Following God's way is not designed to deny you what is good, but to enable you to receive what is best.

Is abstaining from masturbation worth it?

There is no doubt that choosing to glorify God by abstaining from masturbation is not an easy road. In such a sexually saturated society the very concept of radical sexual purity can be daunting and seemingly impossible. But, if God says it is good, you can be sure it will be worth it.

There is nothing greater in life than an intimate relationship with your Creator. It's what you were designed for and it's what can most fulfil you. Unfortunately this can seem hard to believe because of how rarely you may experience it. The junk of this world and the sin of our hearts can infiltrate us so deeply and fill us with self-absorption and shame. These things prevent us from thriving in our relationship with God. Men who have chosen to walk the path of abstaining from masturbation have testified that they feel freer in their relationship with God. The pleasure of intimacy with God does gradually enable them to overcome their desire for personal, physical gratification.

Abstaining from masturbation is also worth it for the effects it can have on your future (or current) marriage. When a person chooses to get their sexual gratification only from their husband or wife, that person becomes more precious, and the act more sacred. When a wife knows that her husband has chosen to receive sexual gratification from her only, the importance of her role increases. They must be willing to serve their spouse in this way, and often are, because they don't have the shame of having to compete. A sexual relationship, in which each is giving to the other exclusively and as an act of service, thrives. It flourishes as a result of being exactly the way God designed it to be.

One of the reasons that abstaining from masturbation can seem so daunting is because of the overwhelming need that so many people feel for it. The thought of depriving oneself of this form of sexual gratification without any immediate hope of fulfilling it rightfully can be very discouraging. Like any habit, however, the longer you refrain from doing it, the easier it becomes. The need to masturbate may seem like a relentless beast at first, but over time, as you commit to glorifying God with your body, and reserving sexual pleasure for your spouse, it becomes easier to control.

The call

This chapter has been extremely difficult to write because we (Sarah and I) wanted to make sure that we were not putting a burden on other people's consciences. Some Christians have told me that, for them, masturbation is not a big problem. They may occasionally masturbate, apparently never to illicit material and it is just something physical. Their consciences are never violated and it never seems to lead them into sexual enslavement. If that is you, then I would urge you to humbly search the Scriptures and seek God's truth. We cannot see that any sexual acts that fall outside of God's design in marriage are condoned or allowed in Scripture, and we fear that you are deceiving yourselves and embracing something that is sinful.

Most people that we have spoken to, however, testify that masturbation is far from harmless. They habitually masturbate, and whether they do it to illicit material or not, they live constantly filled with guilt and shame in their consciences. If you are one of these people I want to give you the following Biblical instruction on how to break free from a pattern of habitual sinful masturbation.

The first step is to renew your understanding of sex. You must embrace a God-centred view of sex and masturbation. What does this mean? First, it means acknowledging that sex is a gift from

God and that your sexuality was created by God. Because He is the one who created it, He is the only One with the authority to dictate how it should be expressed. Therefore, it means dedicating your sex life to him. It means that you must determine that the entirety of your sexual behaviour will be an expression of your honour, love, and fear of Him.

Now you might say, as a reader of my blog said: 'That is great for you, Timon, but I am single and I have strong sexual desires, what am I to do? Take cold showers for the rest of my life?' God has called his people to a high standard of sexual purity, but He is also the provider of the means by which we can achieve that to which He calls us. The provision that God has made for all of us to control our desires is the person of the Holy Spirit. As I said earlier, the reason that we sin is because of strong sinful desires that flow from our hearts. Christ, however, has not left us as orphans but has given us a warrior who can fight for us. Paul tells us that the Holy Spirit wages war against the desires of our sinful nature (Galatians 5:17), and he tells us that by walking by the Spirit we will be able to overcome and not gratify the desires of our sinful natures (Galatians 5:16). This means that by the Spirit we have the ability not to give in to the desire to look at pornographic material and masturbate. We can actually live a life in which our sexual desires (even strong ones) are under control (Galatians 5:23).

Also, from a married man's perspective, let me tell you that things don't always pan out just how you'd like. Just because you are married does not mean that you have access to sex any time you desire it. Even as a married person you will struggle with purity. Many married people struggle with habitual masturbation just like single people. And so, if you marry, you will need the Spirit's empowering just as much as when you were single. All of us need to daily confess our sins to God, surrender our lives to Christ and ask the Holy Spirit for His filling to help us produce His fruit.

On a very practical note, here are several things to help you follow God's call to sexual purity in the area of masturbation:

- Seek the Lord on this issue and develop a strong conviction. When you are tempted you will come up with a dozen reasons why it is okay for you to give in and you need to be able to fight back with the truth of the Scripture and the strength of your conviction.
- Identify the specific times of day and locations in which you're tempted to lust and masturbate. In the morning in my prayer times I spend time praying for the day and asking God to deliver me from temptation. This prepares me in advance for moments of temptation and helps me to develop spiritual alertness.
- Memorize key Scriptures. One of the things that the Holy Spirit will use to produce self-control will be the Word that he inspired. One of my professors at seminary, Howard Hendricks, said that one of the things he gets men who are struggling with purity to do, is to memorize Scripture. If Scripture is filling your mind then there will be less room for other tempting thoughts. 1 Thessalonians 4: 3–6 are some great verses to start with (they speak about learning how to control your own body in a way that is holy and honourable).
- Meditate on Scripture and spend time in prayer and praise of God as you fall asleep. Night-time is probably when you will be tempted most.
- Get out of bed in the morning as soon as your alarm goes off. Lying in bed and allowing your mind to wander is a recipe for failure.

- In moments of temptation, redirect your attention and do something else. Get out of your room, go for a walk, or call a friend.
- Be disciplined about your time in the bathroom and any reading material you keep there.
- Don't play the 'I'll touch myself but won't climax' game. Flee temptation by not touching yourself at all.
- Share your struggle with someone else. Sharing your struggle with a parent or trusted Christian friend is one of the best ways to overcome masturbation.
- Fill your time with activities that put your focus on serving and caring for others.
- Focus on the Gospel. Consistently read Scripture and books that remind you of Christ's sacrifice for your sins. You cannot successfully battle any sin apart from an awareness of God's grace.
- If you sin, dust yourself off, confess to the Lord and get back on the pathway of holiness. Don't let one defeat define your life.

Remember, what God desires from his people is obedience from the heart. Masturbation is not your biggest problem. Your biggest problem is a divided heart.

CHAPTER 7

Homosexuality: Finding God's will and strength in same-sex attraction

Timon Bengtson (with Jeremy Wright)

The lights come up on the set of the talk show. A Christian leader has been invited to speak on his church's programs for the poor, but the talk show host, wanting to spice things up a bit, throws the Christian leader a curveball.

'Why does your church support homophobia?' he asks.

All eyes turn to the man as he stumbles around for answers and appears to be thrown by the disapproving stares that he is getting from the audience.

Like a battering ram, the talk show host bombards him with question after question.

'Aren't you just on the wrong side of history?'

'Doesn't the church need to change to keep up with society and relationships nowadays?'

'Isn't this issue just the same as slavery?'

By the end of the segment the Christian leader looks embarrassed and defeated and the audience leaves, more convinced than ever that the views of the church are out-dated; even morally wrong.

The culture

Homosexuality is one of the most contentious issues facing the church today and yet many churches are ill equipped to deal with it. In a recent study on what stops people from exploring Christianity, 44% said that the church's stance on homosexuality would either significantly or completely block them.[1] So, if almost half the people we talk to will turn away from the gospel because of what they *think* the church says and does about homosexuality, then we as the church need to be absolutely certain of what we believe about it. People will turn away for many reasons, but we cannot have people turning away because of our own ignorance and inability to articulate why we believe what we believe.

Further, many people experience same-sex attraction and we need to be able to minister to them. According to research from La Trobe University, around 2.5% of Australians identify as homosexual or bisexual. However, the percentage of people who have experienced feelings of attraction to those of the same gender or who have had some sexual experience with the same gender is significantly higher (8.6% for men and 15% for women).[2] So statistically, it is likely that there are people in the church for whom this topic is deeply personal.

Maybe this issue is deeply personal for you. Maybe you have struggled with this issue for years and have not found the church to be a safe place to express your struggles and feelings.

Sadly, some of the ways in which the church in general has responded to this issue have not always been helpful. Firstly, many churches and Christians are just ignoring the issue. They are burying their heads in the sand and are trying to pretend that it is still the 1960s. Obviously, this approach will not work. I will never forget sitting one day with a young man who was experiencing same-sex attraction. Unfortunately, when he told his church about his desires, instead of embracing him, loving him and helping him, they asked him to leave. They could not handle what he had to say. I wonder if he had have told them that he was struggling with pornography or masturbation, whether things would have been different.

Other Christians try to 'cure' people of their same-sex attraction. While I think that many ex-gay ministries have been judged harshly, I think we have to admit that in our zealousness to help people we have often approached the issue very simplistically, looking for 'causes' and offering 'cures' that have not been helpful. Rather than seeing same-sex attraction as desires that one may struggle with for life, it has been viewed as simply a result of environmental factors or one's own choice. These approaches have left many struggling people imprisoned and feeling worse. ‡

However, another approach is even more dangerous. Some Christians are capitulating to our culture and are urging Christians to accept homosexuality as normal and healthy. Although this movement seems to be relatively small, as the cultural pressure builds on Christians and churches to conform, I am anticipating it will increase. For example, Rob Bell, a highly acclaimed Christian

---

‡ Michael Brown, in his book on homosexuality, *A Queer thing Happened to America*, devotes an entire chapter, 'The ex-gay movement, fact or fiction', addressing this highly politicised issue.

author, leader and speaker recently came out in favour of the church recognizing committed homosexual relationships. In a radio interview on the UK's premier Christian radio program, *Unbelievable*, Rob Bell was debating Andrew Wilson over the issue. Even though he seemed unwilling to answer some of Wilson's questions about how he interpreted the Scriptures on this issue, his basic response was this: 'Some people are gay and want to share their life with someone, and they should be able to. And that's how the world is and we should affirm that. And we should affirm monogamy, fidelity and commitment, both gay and straight.[3]

Others, like Steve Chalke, a Baptist minister from the UK, try to legitimize homosexuality by appealing to context. They reason that the homosexual prohibitions in the Bible are speaking to a context that is completely different to our own.[4] It is an attractive argument and one that would seem to win favour with the culture, but just because something is favourable does not mean it is right. As we endeavour to discern God's will in this area, we must first ask, 'What does the Bible teach on this topic?'

The Scripture

Is homosexuality a sin?

This of course is the big question. Is homosexuality something that is normal, or something that is forbidden by God in His Word? The place to start to answer this question is not with the prohibition passages in the Bible but rather, with what the Bible presents as God's sexual ideal for humanity. In the beginning we read that God created two genders, male and female (Genesis

1:27-28). In Genesis 2 God said, 'It is not good that the man should be alone; I will make him a helper fit for him' (Genesis 2:18). God then makes Adam fall into a deep sleep and takes a rib from his side. And what does he create for the man so that he will not be alone? It is a woman.

After Adam awakens and expresses his joy at what God has done, the author of Genesis then applies God's provision of Eve for Adam to all marriages. He says, 'Therefore a man shall leave his father and his mother and hold fast to his wife, and they shall become one flesh' (Genesis 2:24). 'One flesh' here refers to sexual union and thus this text establishes the pattern for marriage and sexuality that is taught throughout the rest of the Bible (Cf. Ephesians 5:22-26). Men and women were created for one another and sexual expression is to be inside marriage. As Wayne Grudem points out, sex is the union of the two 'constituent parts of a sexual whole. It is not another man who is the missing part or sexual complement of a man, but rather a woman'.[5] Therefore, His will is that sexuality be expressed between a woman and a man, exclusively in marriage, for life. Any action outside of God's design is a result of the fall and the Bible calls it sin. This, therefore, must include homosexuality.

The 'clobber' passages

While the Genesis model shows homosexuality to be outside God's original design, several passages of Scripture also directly prohibit homosexual practice. Defenders of homosexual practice refer to these passages as the 'clobber passages' because of the way Christians seem to wield them like a weapon to 'clobber' anyone who disagrees. That should be a warning to us to tread carefully, to consider the impact these texts have on people struggling with same-sex attraction (SSA) and to consider how we might use them *well* (without the clobber).

Let's briefly look at these texts and the conclusions we can draw from them.

Genesis 19 & Judges 19

Genesis 19 deals with the story of God's judgment on the city of Sodom. Two angels visit Sodom. Lot sees them and invites them to stay in his house. While there, the men of Sodom 'both young and old, all the people to the last man, surrounded the house' (v4).

They call to Lot to bring out the two men so that they 'may know them' (v5). 'Knowing them' is a euphemism for having sex with them. It's clear from the context that this is the case, because Lot (incredulously) offers them to do as they please to his virgin daughters instead (v8). The men of Sodom clearly wanted these visitors for sex. God's wrath is poured out on the city of Sodom and it is destroyed.

For many, this has been used as a damning judgment on homosexual practice. It seems clear enough on the face of it, but there are some who disagree.

Some have said that the *true* sin of the people of Sodom was failure to show hospitality to the travellers. However, even if this were the case, this does not in any way mean that acting out their lust for the same gender was not also their sin. Indeed, Jude condemns Sodom and Gomorrah for their sexual immorality. Jude 1:7 states, 'just as Sodom and Gomorrah and the surrounding cities, which likewise indulged in sexual immorality and pursued unnatural desire, serve as an example by undergoing a punishment of eternal fire'.

It is clear in the narrative that the homosexual sex that the men of Sodom are seeking is violent and non-consensual. Such violence is just as abhorrent to the average lesbian or gay person as it is to the average heterosexual reader.

A parallel narrative plays out in Judges 19 with the sin of Gibeah. Here the men of the city seek to rape a male Levite visitor to this Benjaminite town. Again, the narrative deals only with a violent expression of homosexuality.

While it is clear that these practices were abominable, these passages probably cannot stand alone as an indictment on all forms of homosexual practice.

Leviticus 18:22 & 20:13

These passages in Leviticus give us further clarity in interpreting God's view of homosexual practice.

Leviticus 18:22 commands that 'You shall not lie with a male as with a woman; it is an abomination', and Leviticus 20:13 states that 'If a man lies with a male as with a woman, both of them have committed an abomination; they shall surely be put to death; their blood is upon them'.

These two texts could not be clearer.

The confusion comes, however, when we consider their relevance to us in a different cultural context and as Christians set free from the law. Sandwiched between these two laws are some other very odd laws: 'Don't eat fruit from a three year old tree' (19:23), 'Don't trim the edges of your beard' (19:27). Most of us don't observe those verses, so why would we observe these two concerning men having sex with men?

Well, even though the surrounding context contains national laws that God gave to Israel, these two verses about homosexuality are embedded in lists of abhorrent sexual practices including incest and bestiality. They are *moral laws* for sexual purity. Leviticus includes three types of law—moral, civil and ceremonial and the Jews understood the differences between them.

- ○ *Moral law* – These dictate an individual's personal responsibility before God and man and are based on God's holy character.
- ○ *Civil law* – These were the unique responsibilities of Israel as a chosen nation before God.
- ○ *Ceremonial law* – These refer to the sacrifices and festivals that God commanded Israel to observe in their worship.

As Christians we would affirm that the laws in Leviticus that refer to the civic obligations of Israel no longer apply to us. We would also affirm that Christ has fulfilled the ceremonial law and that no longer applies to us, however, Christians have always affirmed that God's moral law is still binding.

Further, when we look to the New Testament we find that it continues to prohibit homosexuality.

Romans 1:18-32

This is possibly the clearest passage in the New Testament that articulates God's views on homosexual practice. Here Paul uses the existence of gay and lesbian practice as a clear example of how people have totally turned from the truth and ignored God.

Some would argue that this passage is condemning those who give up heterosexual desires for homosexual actions (exchanging natural relations for those contrary to their nature). But this is really clutching at straws to make a point.

In Romans 1, homosexual practice is a sign of people's rejection of God. It is described as dishonorable, shameful, and impure. It is a sin.

1 Corinthians 6:9-10 & 1 Timothy 1:8-11

Further in both of these above passages it seems clear that Paul is declaring that homosexuality is a sin. Some would argue that the words that Paul employs only refer to unequal homosexual relationships between master and servant, or a man and boy. However, these interpreters are in the minority. Most biblical scholars agree that since that Paul was a Jew, and would have held to the prohibitions from Leviticus, that he was prohibiting any homosexual activity in these verses. So the Bible does teach that homosexual practice is sinful. This is clear both from the positive endorsement of sex within heterosexual marriage as being God's created order for human sexuality, and from the passages that directly prohibit homosexual practice in both the Old and the New Testaments.

Jesus and homosexuality

Many try to cloud the discussion by arguing that since Jesus didn't speak about homosexuality directly, He wouldn't condemn it.

But this argument is flawed. Even though Jesus never directly prohibited homosexuality He did speak very discursively about sexual immorality, homosexuality being included in this category. Further, in Matthew 19, when asked about divorce Jesus affirmed the basic Genesis model for sexuality and marriage.

The easiest assumption on Jesus being mute on homosexuality is that He had nothing to add or take from the law. It makes more sense to assume that if He wanted to change it, He would have taken action and said something, and not stayed silent. If Jesus had endorsed homosexuality, then you would expect His apostles to be just as vocal in endorsing it. This is simply not the case.

Are people born gay?

One of our biggest questions in this area is whether people are born with same-sex desires, or not. One main reason why many people embrace homosexuality as normal, healthy human behaviour is because they believe science has proven that people are born gay. If people are born this way, then who are we to judge them and say that their behaviour is wrong? However, the claim that science has proven people are born gay is very misleading, because the scientific community has not yet reached a consensus concerning the origin of same-sex attraction.

The Bible, however, does not leave us in the dark as to the origin of same-sex attraction. In Romans 1, Paul tells us that all of our sinful desires come from the fall of humanity; that as human beings we 'exchanged the glory of the immortal God for images resembling mortal man and birds and animals and creeping things' (v23). The result of our idolatry is that 'God gave [humanity] up in the lusts of their hearts to impurity, to the dishonouring of their bodies among themselves' (Romans 1:24). Paul further states that God gave them up to dishonourable passions and explains how women exchanged natural relations with men for unnatural relations with other women, and how men exchanged natural relations with men for what is unnatural (Romans 1:26-27). In other words, same-sex attraction and its resultant practice came from the idolatry of humanity and God giving humanity over to follow the lustful desires of their hearts.

Now, people who struggle with same-sex attraction should not read these passages and think that because they have these desires, God has given up on them and they are beyond hope. Here, Paul is talking in general terms about humanity. Later in Chapter 1, he will write that because humans did not see fit to honour God, He gave them up 'to a debased mind to do what ought not to be done' (Romans 1:28). He then outlines a list of sinful desires that flow out of the heart of humanity, stating 'they are full of envy, murder, strife, deceit, maliciousness. They are gossips, slanderers, haters of God, insolent, haughty, boastful, inventors of evil, disobedient to parents, foolish, faithless, heartless, ruthless' (Romans 1:29-31).

There is no living person who can't identify with at least one thing on that list. In other words, every person, as a part of fallen humanity, has a heart that is sinful. In some people these desires will manifest themselves in envy, deceit and malice. In others, it will manifest itself in same-sex attraction.

Now, because of the fall, this disordering of our desires is part of our nature. We are born with sinful natures and hearts that want to sin. So in one sense, you could say that someone was born with desires for same-sex attraction—they were born with a sinful heart that desires to have sex with a person of the same gender.

This does not leave us in a hopeless situation, however, but it does give us a few choices. We can, like some Christians, redefine sin and tell people that homosexuality is okay. But if God has said that homosexuality is a sin, then we are lying to them. Further, we are setting these people up for a life of disobedience to the revealed will of God.

Another option is to just tell people to stop sinning and stop having those desires. But if we do this we may be setting them up for a life of spiritual failure. We are giving them God's standard but are not giving them the power to overcome their desires and fulfil His standard.

A third option is to point them to the power of the gospel. You see the amazing truth of the gospel is that not only does God through Christ provide forgiveness for our sin, but He also transforms our nature giving us the power to overcome our sin. Through the gospel we are given a new nature that desires righteousness. That does not mean that the road ahead will be easy. Sin still resides in our members and we will struggle with a divided heart. It means that for people who struggle with same-sex attraction the battle will be difficult and may last a lifetime. However, the truth of the gospel is that you are not the person you used to be. This is what Paul teaches in 1 Corinthians 6:9-11. Although, he states very plainly that those who practice homosexuality will not inherent the Kingdom of God, he goes onto say to the Corinthians and 'such were some of you' (v11). It is highly likely that in the church in Corinth there were people who had been involved in homosexuality before they became Christians. But Paul goes on to write, 'but you were washed, you were sanctified, you were justified in the name of the Lord Jesus Christ and by the Spirit of our God' (v11). In other words, Paul says you have been changed by the gospel. So even though it will be difficult, God has given us the resources through His Son to live a life pleasing to His will.

The call

In John 4, Jesus was travelling home from Judea. He and His disciples stopped at a Samaritan well in the heat of the day. A woman came to the well and He engaged her in conversation, asking for a drink. As the conversation developed, He made a startling statement:

> Jesus said to her, 'Go, call your husband, and come here'. The woman answered him, 'I have no husband'. Jesus said to her, 'You are right in saying, "I have no husband"; for you have had five husbands, and the one you now have is not your husband. What you have said is true' (v16-18).

This woman had come to the well in shame, in the middle of the day, on her own. She was driven by her own sexual identity. The manner in which she had acted out her sexual desires had left her in a place of shame and compromise.

Notice that Jesus knew what she had done but did not avoid her. He listened to her. He answered her questions. He got to the heart of her problem. And then He revealed Himself as the answer to her problem. 'Whoever drinks of the water that I will give him will never become thirsty again. The water that I will give him will become in him a spring of water welling up to eternal life' (John 4:14).

After exposing all her sexual sin, Jesus revealed to her that He is the Messiah, the Christ.

This woman, whose sexual identity caused her to shy away from everyone, met with Jesus. Everything she'd done was exposed to Him. Yet He *still* offered her living water.

Her reaction is dramatic. She leaves her water jar right there and runs back into town and says to everyone, 'Come and see a man who told me all that I ever did!'(v29) Her shame is gone. Her identity is no longer tied to her sexual activities. Her identity is now bound up in what this man Jesus has just done for her.

The world wants to define us by our sexual desires. It wants to put us in a box labelled 'gay', 'lesbian', 'straight', 'bi', 'fluid' or 'trans'. It demands that we must not suppress these desires, but embrace them, own them, label ourselves with them and act them out. Apparently, only then are we being true to ourselves. I've seen it over and over, how vehemently opposed many are to the thought of people exercising restraint over their desires. The world demands that we let our sexual desires dictate our identity.

Though the world calls us to define ourselves by our desires, Jesus Christ offers us far greater freedom. He does not define us by our sexual desires or actions. He looks past this. He redefines us by His desire for us. To those who come to Jesus in repentance and faith, He calls his own, adopted as children of God (Ephesians 1:5) and members of His household! (Ephesians 2:19)

This is a key truth regarding this issue. Our desires are not our identity. Our identity is bound up in Christ. If He is our Lord, then we let Him define our identity. And the call to follow Christ means a call to die to yourself, take up your cross and follow Him. For people who struggle with same-sex attraction this means an acceptance of His view of their sexuality and a willingness to enter the battle that goes along with it.

Listen to these words from Sam Allberry:

> Ever since I have been open about my own experiences of homosexuality, a number of Christians have said something like this: 'the gospel must be harder for you than it is for me', as though I have more to give up than they do. But the fact is that the gospel demands *everything* of *all of us*. If someone thinks the gospel has somehow slotted into their life quite easily, without causing any major adjustments to their lifestyle or aspirations, it is likely that they have not really started following Jesus at all.[6]

This may seem shocking, but just because someone accepts Christ, it doesn't mean that their desires automatically change. Some desires will change; others we will need to fight against. There are many people who experience SSA, yet cling to Christ and long to live pure and holy lives. What should they do?

1. Pray

Talk to God about how you are feeling and find empathy in Jesus Christ who is able to sympathise with our weaknesses (Hebrews 4:15). Jesus sat with that woman at the well, knowing all her sin. And He listened. That is the same Jesus you serve.

Confess your sins to him knowing that 'If we confess our sins, he is faithful and just to forgive us our sins and to cleanse us from all unrighteousness' (1 John 1:9).

2. Think about yourself in the right way

As Christians, we all need to work on seeing ourselves as God sees us, rather than as the world sees us. If you struggle with SSA, you need to understand the following two points.

Your feelings do not disqualify you. In Christ we are presented holy and blameless in God's sight (Colossians 1:22). Temptation does not disqualify us.

Your feelings do not define you. After listing the characteristics of the unrighteous, Paul says, in 1 Corinthians 6:11, 'and such *were* some of you. But you were washed, you were sanctified, you were justified in the name of the Lord Jesus Christ and by the Spirit of our God'. You take the name of the Lord Jesus Christ. *That* is what now defines you.

In fact, many Christians have found it helpful to use the term 'same-sex attraction' rather than labels such as 'gay', 'lesbian', 'bi', 'queer', 'fluid' or 'trans'. Same-sex attraction refers to feelings only. It doesn't need to suggest that someone who is same-sex attracted acts out those feelings.

This way we are labeling people's feelings and not fixing a label to their identity.

3. Seek the support of others

This is not something to bear on your own. Galatians 6:2 calls on us to bear one another's burdens. In fact, we are charged to keep each other on track.

Brothers, if anyone is caught in any transgression, you who are spiritual should restore him *in a spirit of gentleness*. Keep watch on yourself, lest you too be tempted. Bear one another's burdens, and so fulfill the law of Christ (Galatians 6:1-2).

Be among God's people, fixing your mind on Jesus Christ alongside others. Don't struggle with this alone. It's not good to be alone!

4. Be sexually pure

All those calls to sexual purity are for you, as much as anyone else. With your identity now found in Christ, pursue sexual purity in the strength God provides.

Supporting those with same-sex attraction.

While there are many battles that people struggling with SSA must fight within themselves, there are also a lot of things that the church can do to support them.

1. Recognize the challenges facing Christians struggling with SSA

Christians dealing with SSA have a big battle to face. Sam Allberry lists three main struggles that they commonly have: loneliness, isolation and sexual temptation.[7]

Recognising these, we need to care for the needs of those among us with SSA. The body of Christ is the perfect place to nurture and grow a person struggling with loneliness, isolation and temptation.

We need to recognize what they are giving up in leaving their old life behind: lovers, the potential for a life partner and a very supportive community.

We need to recognise these sacrifices and consider how we as the body of Christ can meet the needs that those sacrifices create.

We need to love Christians struggling with SSA, be their family, and be their friends.

Most importantly, we need to encourage them that their identity is not to be found in their desires, but in Jesus' desire for them!

2. Banish homophobia

Homophobia is reacting to homosexuality poorly. It is being offensive or rude with regard to homosexuality. It is creating an 'us and them' culture.

Colossians 3:8 calls us to put away obscene talk, malice and slander. The Christian community needs to guard itself against such things. The Bible is clear that homosexual practice is a sin. When we speak out about this, others in the community might wrongly interpret this as homophobia. It doesn't have to be. We should let our conversation always be gracious, seasoned with salt, so that we may know how to answer each person (Colossians 4:6).

There is no place for coarse joking about homosexuality in the church. There is no place for the use of the word 'gay' as a derogatory term. We are above that. Guard your speech.

Every time a representative of the body of Christ speaks or acts in a manner that could genuinely be deemed homophobic, more lost people turn away from dialogue with the gospel. It then becomes much harder for the church to engage the world on this issue.

If we seek to be a place of support, openness and safety for people with SSA (and we should), then we must strive to give these precious people no reason to raise their defences against us.

3. Cultivate a high view of singleness

The Bible's call to purity may mean that some people struggling with SSA will be called to a life of singleness. So we need to stop treating singleness as a transitional stage of life, a waiting room for marriage.

Singleness should be celebrated, not downplayed. As Peter Hubbard writes in *Love into Light*, 'Single Christians living in purity and community are billboards for the sufficiency of Jesus'. [8]

Think about this: if we effectively support people with SSA in their pursuit of Biblical sexual purity, they will be such a billboard to the world, a light shining in the darkness, a people who have found a life so much richer than one driven by selfish desires.

Let's start with those within the church who are living with SSA. Let's love them well. Maybe as we do that, we can better engage those outside the church who also experience SSA. Then perhaps this issue might not be such a belief blocker to people, but an opportunity for these SSA saints to shine their light brighter than the world could ever imagine!

CHAPTER 8

The gospel of grace: Finding forgiveness and reclaiming purity

Timon Bengtson

Justine knew she had made mistakes, but they'd begun so long ago, she hardly knew how to do things differently. Her first sexual encounter happened when she was fifteen. Her relationship with her first boyfriend had been physical from the beginning; they'd done just about everything but have sex. In high school, that was just the done thing, and Justine didn't want him to think she was a prude. One night they were at home while her parents were out and in the heat of passion, Justine finally succumbed to her boyfriend's advances. She was usually the one to maintain their boundaries, but this time, she did not resist. Even though she knew that what she was doing was wrong, it was exciting and she wanted more. What she didn't realize, was that she had opened a door that would haunt her for the rest of her life.

The next day Justine felt flooded with guilt and condemnation. She was no longer a virgin. She could no longer look her future husband in the face and say that he was the only person to ever see her naked. She broke down and cried. She could not sleep for days. Then something happened to make it even worse. Her boyfriend, annoyed by the strange way she was acting, dumped her. She'd given him everything, and now she felt used.

Since that time Justine found herself trapped in a vicious cycle. Though she didn't have many boyfriends, she always ended up sleeping with them. She never intended on going that far, but each relationship would follow an inevitable trajectory. First, they would start dating and pretty soon after they would begin a physical relationship. Things would get very serious, very quickly. Then one night, in the grip of passion they would go too far and end up sleeping together.

Justine would inevitably wake up the next morning feeling incredibly guilty. She would spend the next day mentally chastening herself. How could she have done it again? She was raised in a Christian home and knew what the Bible said about sex. What would her parents say? What would her Pastor say? What would the other young people at church say if they knew what she had done? Would the Worship Pastor kick her off the team?

She promised God that she wouldn't do it again. She tried harder and read her Bible more so she would be a 'better' Christian. She told her boyfriend that they needed to promise to never do it again.

Justine wanted to do things right, but this was now her third serious boyfriend and they had fallen into the same sin. She started wondering if there was any hope. Was she destined to make the same mistake over and over again? Would there ever be freedom from this sin? Could her guilty conscience ever be cleansed? Could she ever overcome the shame of knowing that she was no longer a virgin?

The culture

Maybe this is a question that you have been asking yourself as you have read through this book. You may have sinned, like Justine, by having sex before you are married, or struggle with pornography, masturbation or same-sex attraction and you have tried to live God's way, but it is just not working. And maybe you are filled with remorse, shame and guilt, and wonder if there is any hope for you? Can you live a life of sexual purity that God outlines in His word? Can you live a life of pure love?

Well, there is hope, and it is found in unwrapping the gift of grace that you were given when you first believed the gospel. It may be hard to believe, but you already have all you need for a life of freedom and joy in Christ. The Apostle Peter states that, 'His divine power has granted to us all things that pertain to life and godliness, through the knowledge of him who called us to His own glory and excellence' (2 Peter 1:3). Notice Peter says, 'has granted'. It is in the past tense. In other words, God's divine power has already, right now, given us all we need to help us overcome our sin and live a life of purity. You already have all the power you will ever need in the gospel to overcome sin and to help you pursue purity. All you need to do is use it.

The Scripture

We all know that external behavioural change is possible. With determination and willpower, a person can stop looking at pornography, but it can be with the completely wrong motivation.

Consider Phil: before he became a Christian he had a hard drive full of pornographic movies and images that he had downloaded. As soon as he became a Christian, he realized that these needed to go. In order to help him in his struggle, he joined an accountability group of guys who would give a report on their progress each week. The guys would get together, ask each other questions and then chastise or praise one another according to how they had gone. Phil had been a very good sportsman and had been good academically at school, so he was very eager to please and had a competitive streak that motivated him to do well. He determined early on that he was not going to be like Ryan, who came each week with the same story of defeat. And so every week, he would come and proudly announced that *he had been porn-free* and described the way in which *he had been walking in victory*. Phil had changed his behaviour, he was no longer looking at porn, but had his heart changed in a way that was honouring to God? Is internal heart change really possible? [§]

You see there are actually two types of ways to change: religious change and gospel change.[**]

Religious change

In religious change, the motivation for change is to look good externally. It is to show others, often for our own pride, how great a Christian we are. In religious change, the power for change is

---

[§]   I am not inferring that an accountability group is a bad thing. In fact, change is a community project. The lone Christian is a dead Christian. But what we have to watch out for is accountability groups that have at their heart a legalistic model of change. Note what Jonathan Dodson says, 'Although accountable relationships start with a noble aim—commitment to confession, encouragement, and prayer for one another—they often devolve into relationships based on rule keeping or rule breaking. The religious verbally punish others for failing to keep the rules, while the rebellious are quick to overlook one another's failure. Both are rule centered' If you want to investigate this topic further, look at Dodson, Jonathan K (2012-03-31), *Gospel-centered discipleship* (Re:Lit) (p. 64), Crossway, Kindle Edition.

[**]   I am using 'religion' here in a pejorative way to describe a legalistic man-centred approach to change. Of course, Christianity can be classed as a religion.

our own will. We believe that if we can just get our act together and make the right decisions then we will change. Further, religious change makes us believe that the reason God accepts us is because of our performance.

But the problem with religious change is threefold:

1. **It will not drive the love of sin out of our hearts**. Our biggest problem when it comes to sexual immorality is that we love it. JD Greear writes, 'At its root, our sins are driven by the fact that we desire something more than we desire God.'[1] We sin because in that moment we want something more than God.

2. **It tends to promote pride and self-loathing**. If you believe that your acceptance with God is based upon your performance, then when you are doing well, you will be filled with pride. You may even look down on other Christians who cannot control their sexual appetites and wonder why they can't get it together. However, when you do slip up and sin, you will find that, like Justine, you go into a deep pit of self-loathing and mental criticism, unable to handle what you have just done. Heath Lambert, in his book *Finally free* says this on the topic of pornography:

> Mental punishments are not helpful because they deal with sin in a self-centred way instead of a Christ-centred way. Meditating on how miserable and pathetic you are only perpetuates the sinful self-centeredness that led you to look at pornography in the first place. Condemning self-talk still has you standing centre stage as you reflect on what you think about what you have done, and as you describe what you think you deserve because of what you did. It's all about you. The problem is there is too much you in all this. You need Christ.[2]

It seems strange to think that self-criticism can be self-centred, but as Lambert said, when we make it all about us, we're ignoring Christ. When we try to self-atone, we're trying to take the place of the Saviour in our lives.

3. **Religious change makes us resent God rather than love Him.** When we try to change in our own strength, God becomes someone we can never please or satisfy. Further, we find that we can never rest, because we never know if we have done enough to be worthy of His love and forgiveness. In the end, many who pursue change through religion find themselves like the older brother in the parable 'The prodigal son' (Luke 15:11-32). They are unable to enter their father's celebration of his younger son's return and they become angry that the Father would even stoop so far as to offer grace to the undeserving.

Gospel change

Gospel change, on the other hand, works on a completely different paradigm to religious change. The gospel changes us by changing our hearts. The gospel announces that through the death and resurrection of Jesus, all our past, present and future sin has been forgiven and we are presently and permanently standing before Him in love as His sons and daughters. It announces that through our union with Christ, sin's power over our nature has been broken and we have received the gift of the Holy Spirit, who is renewing us daily into the image of Christ. Finally, the gospel promises that one day, when Christ returns, our fight with sin will be over and we will be made completely righteous.

Therefore it is the Gospel that provides the platform for our change.

1. **The gospel has the power to drive out the root idolatries from our hearts, and turn us into a worshipper of the true God.** As previously discussed, the reason that we sin is because we love it; we desire something more than God. But unlike 'religion,' the gospel has the power to capture our hearts, because in the gospel we behold the magnitude of God's love for us through Christ. As we do this, our hearts become enflamed with love for God. John says, 'we love because He first loved us' (1 John 4:19). The more we believe and behold the love of God in the gospel, the more we come to truly believe that God's love in Christ is all we need for everlasting joy and security. This helps us to turn from sin and its deception, and turn to God and embrace Him. As we continually focus and depend on Jesus and His work for our acceptance with God, we will find new desires for holiness starting to grow in our hearts. As we follow through on those desires with obedience we will find the character of Jesus starting to form in our lives.

2. **God's acceptance and forgiveness means that I run *to* Him, not *away* from Him, when I sin.** When we sin, we are all prone to run away from God and hide. Like our first parents, we tend to believe that we cannot approach God until we have at least cleaned ourselves up a bit and covered our nakedness with a few good works. But this is not the teaching of the gospel. The gospel means that Christ has suffered the full wrath of God for my sin and that through His death I am completely forgiven, justified, reconciled and accepted. Justification means my guilt—not my guilty feeling,

but my actual guilt—has been acquitted (Romans 5:1). I am standing before God in the righteousness of Christ.

Now if I believe that I am completely forgiven of all my sin, instead of running away from Christ when I sin, I should run to Him. Not proudly, or arrogantly, but humbly confessing my sin and finding the grace that I so desperately need (Hebrews 4:16). It is actually confidence in the ability of the blood of Jesus to forgive and cleanse that enables repentance. If I am confident that Jesus can cleanse and forgive my sin then I will come to Him. It is actually a lack of faith in His ability to forgive and cleanse that leads us to hide and believe that we must develop a bit of a 'track record' before we can turn back to Him.

These things are important to remember because change is slow and takes time. We will fail over and over again. It is unrealistic to think that you will only need to repent one time of your sexual sin. But as you keep repenting and turning back to God because of the assurance that all of your sins have been forgiven by God, you will gradually change.

3. **The gospel gives us the ability to persevere in our fight with sin.** As Christians we must remember that, through the gospel, sin's power has been disarmed. In Romans 6:4 Paul says that 'We were therefore buried with [Christ] through baptism into death in order that, just as Christ was raised from the dead through the glory of the Father, we too may live a new life'. You see Paul is saying that the gospel goes beyond Christ having died for us. It teaches that through our union with Christ, we also died with Christ. As Heath Lambert states:

His death and resurrection is also our death and resurrection. Jesus' death and resurrection not only pays off our record of debt and gives us forgiving grace; Jesus' death and resurrection leads to our transformation.[3]

Many people cry out for Jesus' forgiving grace, but they do not know what to do next. Well, next they need to *claim* His transforming grace. As Paul says, we need to 'consider ourselves' dead to sin and alive to God (Romans 6:11). This means that through the gospel we already have the power to fight sin, we just need to claim it. We don't have to go around wondering whether we have the ability to fight sin in our lives; we already possess that ability through our union with Christ.

4. **And finally, the gospel gives us the hope to persevere to the end.** Some Christians seem to believe that God's only agenda is their temporal happiness, however God is much more interested in our joy in Him and in conforming us to the image of His Son. To achieve this purpose God allows suffering and pain in our lives. For single Christians it may mean having to live with the fact that God has not chosen to bring a spouse into their lives. Or for Christians struggling with same-sex attraction, it may mean struggling with those desires and remaining celibate for the rest of their lives.

These struggles are difficult and painful. They are trials that require strength beyond our own. So where does the hope come from to persevere to the end? Where does the joy come from to keep on pursuing God even when it is difficult? It comes from the gospel. It comes from the assurance that even though it may be tough now, our sufferings are not worth comparing with the glory that will be revealed to us (Romans

8:18). It comes from the assurance that when Christ returns, we will see Him as He is and be changed to be like Him (1 John 3:2). It is this assurance of our future security that gives us joy and hope, and it is God's daily, fresh supply of grace that provides us with the strength to continue in spite of our circumstances.

The call

So how do we appropriate the benefits of the gospel in our lives and really change? It is through repentance and faith. The same way that we came to Christ (by repenting and believing the gospel) is the way that we continue to change. Your whole Christian life will be a journey of turning away from sin and turning to Christ.

The Greek word for repentance is the word *metanoano* and means 'to change your mind'. However, this alone does not capture the essence of what it means to repent. In 2 Corinthians 7:10 Paul says that 'godly grief produces a repentance that leads to salvation without regret'. This verse teaches three phases in the repentance process:

1. **Firstly, there is conviction.** God's Spirit shines His light on your heart and convicts you of your sin and it produces sorrow in your heart; sorrow that you have sinned against God and broken fellowship with him; sorrow that you have misused His grace; sorrow that you have not lived as you should have lived. However, you must be careful because Paul points out that there are two types of sorrow—godly sorrow and worldly sorrow. Heath Lambert states:

Worldly sorrow is obsessed with keeping these objects of selfish desire. All the tears and all the pain are actually about the loss of your stuff. You're crying about the things you're about to lose and would like to keep…. Worldly sorrow is sad over losing the things of the world, while the focus of godly sorrow is God himself. Godly sorrow is pained over the break in relationship with God. It is heartbroken that God has been grieved and offended. The tears of godly sorrow flow from the sadness that God's loving and holy law has been broken.[4]

Further, we must watch for the difference between the voice of the Holy Spirit and the voice of the devil. The Holy Spirit will always come to us in conviction, pointing to specific sins that He wants to change in our lives. The Devil, on the other hand, will pour condemnation on us putting a wet blanket over us so that we will be unable to move.

Charles Price tells this story about a woman that he had met while ministering. She told him that for twenty years she had confessed to God a particular sin that she had been involved in in her late teens. He didn't ask her for the details, but she said that for twenty years—she was now around forty —she had confessed this sin to God every day.

She said, 'The memory of that sin and the consequence of that sin have sat on me the whole of this time. It has impacted my marriage; it's even made me a poor mother to my children'. She told Charles that the church she attended asked her if she would teach a Sunday school class several times because she was very capable with children but she said, 'I have turned it down every time because I know what I'm like, and I know my past. I couldn't possibly serve God because of my history'.[5]

That is not conviction of the Holy Spirit, but rather a prison of condemnation. The devil is very clever. Before you came to Christ he was trying to prevent you from seeing Him but now you are in Christ he is trying to prevent you from embracing Him and the full benefits of your salvation.

While we need to be on the lookout for the devil's condemnation, don't shy away from godly sorrow and the Holy Spirit's conviction over your sin. In fact, John Owen, a puritan writer from the 1600's, wrote that if you want to mortify sin—which is just an old word meaning to kill sin—then what you need to do is 'load your conscience with the guilt of it'.[6] If the Holy Spirit is shining His light on your heart don't harden your heart to His voice, let your heart feel the full weight of His conviction. Listen to the counsel that James 4:8-10 gives us: 'draw near to God and He will draw near to you'. This all sounds positive, doesn't it, but then he goes onto say:

> Cleanse your hands, you sinners; purify your hearts, you double minded. Be wretched and mourn and weep. Let your laughter be turned to mourning and your joy to gloom. Humble yourselves before the Lord, and He will exalt you.

The pathway back to God is one that is paved with tears. John Welch, another 17th century Scottish preacher said:

> There is a godly sorrow which leads a man to life. This sorrow is wrought in a man by the Spirit of God, and in the heart of the godly, that he mourns for sin because it has displeased God, who is so dear and so sweet a Father to him.[7]

2. **The next step in true repentance is to move from conviction to confession.** You feel convicted of your sin

and sorry for your sinful actions and this causes you to go to God and confess your sin. As Paul says in 2 Corinthians 7:10, 'godly sorrow brings repentance', (NIV) that is, godly sorrow produces a complete change of mind in regard to the sin. You go to God and you admit that you have sinned against Him. You admit that it was wrong. You not only confess your sins, but you also confess the ways that you have replaced Him in your life and the idols you have worshipped and served.

However, confession is more than admitting you have sinned, it is also involves affirming you are forgiven. As John states, 'If we confess our sins, He is faithful and just and will forgive us our sins and cleanse us from all unrighteousness' (1 John 1:9). Confession involves believing this to be true—that through the gospel we are forgiven and cleansed. It involves turning to Christ and believing that He is the righteous one standing at the Father's right hand interceding for us. Much repentance fails at this point, because we refuse to believe that Christ has forgiven us. We wallow around mentally chastising ourselves for our sin, instead of looking up to the cross and affirming God's forgiveness.

3. **The final step in the process of repentance is that true repentance produces fruit—a changed life**. George Whitefield once said, 'True repentance will entirely change you; the bias of your souls will be changed, then you will delight in God, in Christ, in His Law, and in His people'.[8] As John the Baptist said to religious people in his day, if there is no fruit produced in keeping with repentance, then repentance means nothing (Matthew 3:8).

Of course, we have not yet been made perfect. We will slip up and there will be much failure. However, as we continue to repent and believe the gospel, fruit will gradually grow in our lives and we will change. You will find that as you draw nearer to the Son and feel the heat of His holiness, it will melt away the hardness of your heart and you will repent. As you continue practising this lifestyle of repentance and faith you will change.

So what is the sexual sin that you are battling with right now? Have you repented of it and are just battling with the temptation? Or are you defeated by it? Even worse, are you hardened to the point where you don't even care anymore? If you are in that place, then you really need to cry out to God the Holy Spirit to bring the heat of His conviction. If you haven't repented then maybe you need to spend some time alone with God. Take time to feel the weight of God's conviction—don't run away from guilt—let your guilt draw you to God for mercy and forgiveness, then confess and forsake your sin, affirm your forgiveness and turn to God to change you.

There is much more that could be said about gospel change that we do not have time to mention. There are many practical steps that can help you maintain purity and assist you in a lifestyle of repentance and faith. We have hopefully given you this practical instruction in the 'Call' sections of each of our chapters. But as we conclude this chapter it is very important to note that change is a community project. Up to this point you might have thought that gospel change is just about you and Jesus. However, nothing could be further from the truth.

God has made us part of His body for a reason. In Ephesians 4:16, we read that the whole body grows as 'it builds itself up in love'. It is assumed that Christians will be members of a church and will grow through their participation. You see as we worship God together, encourage each other, share our struggles with one another, pray for each other and very importantly preach the gospel to each other, we find the strength and support to maintain this lifestyle of repentance and faith.

So if you have taken a particular sin to God and are still struggling with it, you really need to find a trusted mature Christian and ask for their counsel and support. Repentance and faith is nurtured and developed in the context of God's people, the church. The reason you came to Christ was because the church preached the gospel to you and the way that you will continue to grow is through your faith being nurtured by the preaching, worship and support of your local church.

We hope that this book has opened your eyes and convicted your hearts on the many challenges that we all face in regards to our sexuality. We hope that it has empowered you with Scripture and practical ways for you to guard against the temptations that rage rampantly around us, and we hope that it equips you to be a shining beacon of hope, redeeming culture and living as God intended. But mostly we hope that this book will remind you that without Jesus we are nothing, with no hope for change, but that with Him, we have already overcome the world.

May your lives bring glory to Him as you reflect His holiness and embrace His grace in all areas of your sexuality, and may we all, as His church in this time, stand strong in His power, surrendered to His will.

CityReach Baptist Church is a multi-campus church in Adelaide, South Australia.

Our vision is to Gather to exalt Jesus, Grow to become like Jesus, Give to serve like Jesus and Go to share Jesus.

Please visit us at www.cityreach.com.au

REFERENCES

Chapter 1

[1] Jeremy Clark, *I gave Dating a Chance*, Colorado Springs, WaterBrook Press, 2000, p.106.

Chapter 2

[1] Tim Keller (with Kathy Keller), *The Meaning of Marriage*, Kindle Edition, Hodder & Stoughton, 2011, p.110.

[2] R. Morgan, L. Stock, and J. Cavanaugh, *You're nobody til somebody loves you*, 1944.

[3] Whitney Houston (written by David Foster and Linda Tompson), *I have nothing*, Arista, 1993.

[4] Lina Abujamra. *Thrive: The Single Life as God intended*, United States, Moody Publishers, 2013, p. 38.

[5] St. Augustine. *The Confessions*, Peabody, Massachusetts, Hendrickson Publishers, 2004, p. 5.

[6] Lina Abujamra. *Thrive: The Single Life as God intended*, United States, Moody Publishers, 2013, p.28.

[7] Elisabeth Elliot, *Let me be a Woman- Notes to my daughter on the meaning of womanhood*, Carol Stream, Illinois, Tyndale House Publishers, 1999, p.25

[8] Tim Keller (with Kathy Keller), *The Meaning of Marriage*, Kindle Edition, Hodder & Stoughton, 2011, p.107.

[9] Marshall Segal, 'Single, Satisfied and Sent: Mission for the not-yet married', *Desiring God*, [web blog], 13 March 2013, http://www.desiringgod.org/articles/single-satisfied-and-sent-mission-for-the-not-yet-married, (accessed 21 February 2015) Used by permission.

Chapter 3

1   Andreas J. Köstenberger, *God, Marriage and Family: Rebuilding the Biblical Foundation*, Wheaton, Illinois, Crossway Books, 2004, pp.37-38.
2   Hayley DiMarco, *The Woman of Mystery- unveiling the secret to true romance*, Carol Stream, Illinois, Tyndale House Publishers, pp.81-82
3   Hayley DiMarco, *The Woman of Mystery- unveiling the secret to true romance*, Carol Stream, Illinois, Tyndale House Publishers, p83.
4   Jeremy Clark, *I gave Dating a Chance*, Colorado Springs, WaterBrook Press, 2000, p.84.

Chapter 4

1   Christine Dell'Amore, 'Bikinis Make Men See Women as Objects, Scans Confirm', *National Geographic News*, Chicago, 16 February 2009, http://news.nationalgeographic.com.au/news/2009/02/090216-bikinis-women-men-objects.html and Elizabeth Landau, 'Men see bikini-clad women as objects, psychologists say' *CNN*, Chicago, 2 April 2009, http://edition.cnn.com/2009/HEALTH/02/19/women.bikinis.objects.index.html?PHPSESSID=508431b1d8a6454f1b85e358493b4a75
2   John MacArthur, *The MacArthur Study Bible- New King James Version*, Nashville, Word Publishers, 1997, p.1863 (footnotes for 1 Timothy 2:9)
3   Tim Challies and R.W. Glenn, *Modest: Men and Women Clothed in the Gospel*, Adelphi, Cruciform Press, 2012.
4   Tim Challies and R.W. Glenn, *Modest: Men and Women Clothed in the Gospel*, Adelphi, Cruciform Press, 2012, p.12.
5   Eric Ludy and Leslie Ludy, *When God writes your love story- the ultimate guide to guy/girl relationships*, Colorado Springs, Multnomah Books, 2009, p.120.
6   Dannah Gresh, *Secret Keeper: The Delicate Power of Modesty*, Chicago, Moody Publishers, 2002, p.44.
7   Dannah Gresh, *Secret Keeper: The Delicate Power of Modesty*, Chicago, Moody Publishers, 2002, p.19.

Chapter 5

1   Simon Lajeunesse in R. Nauert, 'Pornography's Effect on Men Under Study', *Psych Central*, 2 December 2009, http://psychcentral.com/news/2009/12/02/pornographys-effect-on-men-under-study/9884.html, (accessed 11 February 2014).

2   The UK independent, 29 September 2014. (accessed from: 'Current Porn Statistics', *The Road to Grace*, www.roadtograce.net/current-porn-statistics/ on 8 January 2015)

3   The Oxford Student, 12 June 2014 (accessed from: 'Current Porn Statistics', *The Road to Grace*, www.roadtograce.net/current-porn-statistics/ on 8 January 2015)

4   IFOP Survey Institute, 15 May 2014 (accessed from: 'Current Porn Statistics', *The Road to Grace*, www.roadtograce.net/current-porn-statistics/ on 8 January 2015)

5   Policy Mic 3-9-13 (accessed from: 'Current Porn Statistics', *The Road to Grace*, www.roadtograce.net/current-porn-statistics/ on 8 January 2015)

6   ZeeNews India, May 5, 2013 (accessed from: 'Current Porn Statistics', *The Road to Grace*, www.roadtograce.net/current-porn-statistics/ on 8 January 2015)

7   Tim Challies, *Sexual Detox: A guide for guys who are sick of porn*, Adelphi, Md. Cruciform Press, 2010, p.17.

8   Tim Challies, *Sexual Detox: A guide for guys who are sick of porn*, Adelphi, Md. Cruciform Press, 2010, p.25

9   Tim Challies, *Sexual Detox: A guide for guys who are sick of porn*, Adelphi, Md. Cruciform Press, 2010, p.24

10   abhor. Dictionary.com. *Collins English Dictionary - Complete & Unabridged 10th Edition.* HarperCollins Publishers. http://dictionary.reference.com/browse/abhor (accessed: March 02, 2015).

11   Challies, Tim. *Sexual Detox: A guide for guys who are sick of porn*, Adelphi, Md. Cruciform Press, 2010, p.15

12   Stephen Arterburn and Fred Stoeker, *Every Man's Battle: Winning the War on Sexual Temptation One Victory at a Time*, Colorado Springs, WaterBrook Press, 2009.

13   Heath Lambert, *Finally Free: Fighting for Purity with the Power of Grace*, (Kindle Edition), Zondervan, 2013, p.125.

Chapter 6

1   'Masturbation key to healthy, functional sexual relationships', *The Badger Herald: UW Madison's Premier Independent Student Newspaper*, Madison, Wisconsin, 19 April 2007, http://badgerherald.com/oped/2007/04/19/masturbation-key-to/#.UzUdkF5hurc, (accessed 21 February 2015).

2   James Dobson, *Preparing for Adolescence*, Ventura, California, Vision House, 1978, p.87.

3   R. Albert Mohler, *Desire and Deceit: The real cost of the new sexual tolerance*, Kindle Version, Multnomah Books, 2008, Kindle Locations 877-878.

4   Peter T. O'Brien, *Word Biblical Commentary: Colossians – Philemon*, Vol. 44, Thomas Nelson, 1982, p.181.

5   Jeffrey Black, as quoted in Joshua Harris *Sex is not the problem (lust is): Sexual Purity in a Lust Saturated World*, Kindle Edition, Doubleday, 2009, (Kindle Locations 963-967).

6   Peter T. O'Brien, *Word Biblical Commentary: Colossians – Philemon*, Vol. 44, Thomas Nelson, 1982, p.181.

7   Joshua Harris, *Sex is not the problem (lust is): Sexual Purity in a Lust Saturated World*, Kindle Edition, Multnomah, 2005, p.104.

8   Peter T. O'Brien, *Word Biblical Commentary: Colossians – Philemon*, Vol. 44, Thomas Nelson, 1982, p.182.

9   John Owen, *Overcoming Sin and Temptation*, Wheaton, Illinois, Crossway Books, 2006, p.50.

10 Joshua Harris, *Sex is not the problem (lust is): Sexual Purity in a Lust Saturated World*, Kindle Edition, Multnomah, 2005, p.106.

Chapter 7

1   Australian Communities Report,' *Olive Tree Media*, Research Conducted by McCrindle Research, October 2011, http://www.olivetreemedia.com.au/resources/Olive%20Tree%20Media/Apologetics%20Series/Reseach%20Summary-web.pdf (accessed 2 March 2015).

2   'Sex in Australia: Summary Findings of the Australian study of Health and Relationships,' *LaTrobe University, et.al.* 2003, http://www.dialog.unimelb.edu.au/lesbian/pdf/sex%20in%20australia%20summary%204.03.pdf (accessed 2 March 2015).

3   'Rob Bell and Andrew Wilson // Homosexuality & The Bible // Unbelievable?' *Premier on Demand*, May 3 2013, http://www.youtube.com/watch?v=XF9uo_P0nNI&feature=kp, Quote taken from 1:20, (accessed 2 March 2015)

4   Steve Chalke, *The Bible and Homosexuality*, Premier Christianity, 2013 www.premierchristianity.com/Featured-Topics/Homosexuality/The-Bible-and-Homosexuality-Part-One (accessed 26 February 2015).

5   *ESV Study Bible*, Kindle Version, Wheaton, Illinois, Crossway, 2013, Kindle Location 349525.

6   Sam Allberry, *Is God Anti-gay?* The Good Book Company, UK, 2013. p10.

7   Alburry, Sam, *Is God Anti-gay?* The Good Book Company, UK, 2013. P52-53.

8   Peter Hubbard, *Love into light: the Gospel, the homosexual and the church*, Greenville, South Carolina, Ambassador International, 2013, Kindle Location 1597.

Chapter 8

1   J.D. Greear, *Gospel: Recovering the Power that made Christianity Revolutionary*, Kindle Edition, B&H Publishing Group, 2013, p.30.

2   Heath Lambert, *Finally Free: Fighting for Purity with the Power of Grace*, Kindle Edition, Zondervan, 2013, p.26.

3   Heath Lambert, *Finally Free: Fighting for Purity with the Power of Grace*, Kindle Edition, Zondervan, 2013, pp. 21-22

4   Heath Lambert, *Finally Free: Fighting for Purity with the Power of Grace*, Kindle Edition, Zondervan, 2013, p.35.

5   Charles W. Price, *Christ for Real: How to Grow into God's Likeness*, Kindle Edition, Kegel Publications, 1995, Kindle Locations 933-934.

6   John Owen, *Overcoming Sin and Temptation*, Wheaton, Illinois, Crossway Books, 2006, p.103.

7   As quoted in: C. H. Spurgeon, *The Treasury of David*, Hendrickson Publishers, 1990, p.412

8   George Whitfield, *Sermons*, Fischerts and Jackson, 1832, p.369.

Printed in the United States
By Bookmasters